It's not who

PETER

Veteran Off-Spinner

A light-hearted review of the life of a local cricket
legend through the decades, and the importance of
social connections that have shaped his journey

By
Andrew Oakley

www.publishnation.co.uk

Dedication

To my gorgeous, understanding wife Aggie, who supported my insane idea of writing a book about Dad, and for tolerating my occasional excitement following another revelation about him. Also, to my beautiful daughter Georgie, who recalls Bedford Grandad picking up the phone when she was younger and Dad stating simply: 'It's Pete from Bedford.'

Foreword

Peter Oakley or 'Oakers', as he was known to generations of Bedford Town, Bedford School and Bedfordshire cricketers, has lived a life in cricket.

From his time as a youngster on the Lord's Ground staff to becoming the fierce protector of the kit room in the Bedford School cricket pavilion, a love of the game has characterised all that he has done.

I first met him when I joined Bedford School at the age of the thirteen. Even with all I have been lucky enough to achieve in the game, my days at Bedford are some of my most cherished cricketing memories and Oakers was a constant and reassuring presence throughout.

One of my abiding memories is the arrival of the legendary Derek Randall as the cricket professional for my final years at Bedford.

For a young batsman it was such a thrill for Derek to be our coach, but I believe that Oakers was even more excited.

Oakers and Derek were as thick as thieves. They were drinking buddies and golf partners, and they would spend endless hours talking cricket.

As I made my way into the professional game, with cricket taking me to places I could only ever have dreamed of, I still always looked forward to returning to Bedford, and one reason for that was to catch up with Oakers.

We would share a drink in the De Parys, the famous Bedford hotel, and compare war stories.

Oakers is a true man of cricket. Our great game is built from people like him, whose dedication, enthusiasm, and spirit are truly boundless.

I want to congratulate him on a splendid life in sport and for having this wonderful book written about him. I am sure you will enjoy reading it as much as I have.

Sir Alastair Cook, June 2021

Preface

I recall listening to Sir Clive Lloyd CBE a number of years ago, celebrating the success of the West Indies during the 1970s, referring to cricket as being *more than a game;* that it was about building a wealth of connections on and off the pitch that would shape one's life. That has always resonated with me: Dad's wonderful life has indeed been mapped around strong connections through his love of and dedication to cricket.

From Bluey (Trevor) Thomas building the downstairs loo, Pricey (David) delivering the milk, Fred (Breeze) agreeing to the mortgage advance, through to Davison and Pack (Peter) offering summer jobs for the boys, people helped each other – and they were all *connections* made through the game.

In my younger years, I would scan the local newspapers (delivered via Turners on Goldington Road, back pages read first, just like Dad) looking for references to Dad's weekly cricketing exploits. Even in his forties, Dad was given the 'veteran off-spinner' label, which he always seemed mildly amused by.

More often than not, he would just be another statistic within the overall Bedford Town CC scorecard. I soon realised, however, that P. J. Oakley 'dnb' didn't mean *dignitary and notable Bedfordian,* but simply 'did not bat': an understandable status, given that the team usually contained a wealth of talented batsmen, such as Briggs, Machin, Curtis *et al.*

However, occasionally Dad did grab the headlines: 'Veteran off-spinner grabs 5, as the Town win at Mill Hill'.

Dad was never happier than when sitting down watching Test match cricket on the BBC and listening to Jim Laker and Richie Benaud's commentary. Laker had that distinct, throaty but captivating voice that would have been well served on *Jackanory*, while Benaud's tone, I was convinced, was as a result of taking short puffs from a helium balloon. My role was to ensure that the long, dense, burgundy velvet lounge curtains prevented the sunlight from penetrating and obscuring the picture on the old Pye television.

I can't recall Dad ever questioning me about the adequacy of my homework (that was clearly part of my mum's role), but what was important to him was that Boycott was still at the crease at the close of play!

Research has shown that surrounding yourself with strong social connections lowers anxiety and depression levels. Dad never really over-stressed himself, even during challenging times. At the time of writing, Dad is 87 not out: there aren't too many quick singles these days, although he did decide to hang on to a diving catch last year when playing ball with border collie Millie and has been recuperating since from a few pelvic fractures. It was confirmed that despite his heavy encounter with the concrete patio, the ball did carry!

'I was married to cricket,' the legendary umpire Dickie Bird (who once spoke at the annual Bedford Town CC dinner) told a reporter when asked why he had remained single. If you were to ask my mum the same, I'm confident that she would respond similarly about Dad. His love and affection for the game transcended the Goldington Bury, and has remained a constant throughout his lifetime. The subject of cricket was ever-present in the Oakley household, evidenced by watercolour paintings of Lord's and Bedford School's Old Boys matches displayed on the walls. At birthdays and at Christmas, cards from across the world would litter the house, the majority being cricket-related, and usually containing little updates, or conveying brief stories, such as, 'did you know that . . .' and 'you'll never believe who I came across . . .'

I hope you enjoy reading this series of anecdotal stories through the decades as much as I enjoyed writing the book and engaging with my Dad, his newspaper cuttings, and connections from his playing days to gain the details of a wonderful, fulfilling life underpinned by an infinite love for the game of cricket.

Andrew Oakley, Northampton, June 2021

Thanks

To Mum, for verifying some of the details; Lynn, for her meticulous proofreading; and Dad's cricketing friends Bob Gray, Russell Beard, Colin Head, Mick Meadows, and Mike Green for their valuable contributions.

Contents

The Early Years (1930s/40s)

<u>Suffolk connection</u>
Dad's journey begins in Sudbury, Suffolk: great-grandmother May lived in Long Melford, in deepest 'Constable Country'.

The nearest Dad came to artistic skill was when he was painting the crease, using the 'marking-out frame', or walking around the edge of the cricket outfield, using the old, white transfer line-marker to paint the boundary line.

I remember, as a ten-year-old, watching Dad's trousers gradually getting covered in white lime powder (later on in life I found out that the substance could cause blindness). However, Dad was seemingly bulletproof and resilient: a quality of his that I'll be referring to from time to time.

Dad always seemed to achieve the perfect boundary line, curving each end right in front of the sight screens. Occasionally, when other players stepped in at short notice to assist, the line on the Church Lane side ended up resembling a dog-leg, perhaps as a result of someone still inebriated from the night before.

<u>John and Elsie Oakley</u>
Dad's father, John Oakley (also known as 'Jack'), worked for Eastern National Coaches. The company subsequently became United Counties and moved to Clacton-on-Sea, so Jack moved with his job.

'Bedford Grandad', as we fondly remember him, wasn't into cricket: his passion was cars and motor bikes, and this was no doubt the origin of Dad's own love for cars over the years. One time, Bedford Grandad took my older brother, Stephen, and me to the TT races on the Isle of Man for a long weekend. I remember Bedford Grandad sporting a shirt and tie, with a trilby to finish his smart appearance, standing proud at the famous Goose Neck Bend at Ramsey; the deafening sound of the large bikes, the clouds of fumes and smoke, and the smell of fuel that contrasted with the fresh scent of hay bales.

Bedford Grandad was ahead of his time when it came to re-cycling. Every year, he 'made up' bikes for his two sons: in his later years would make them for Stephen and me. Dad would watch his father working on cars and bikes, and was occasionally allowed to clean down an engine using paraffin and a cloth. He's adamant that this is how he got his lifelong passion for cars.

As Dad entered his teens, Bedford Grandad was running a private car-hire business. At that time, he was overloaded with work, so he would occasionally place a cap on Dad's head, a cigarette in his mouth, and send him off to pick up a client from the other side of town. I now know from where my fun-loving younger brother, Jon, got his audaciousness.

Dad's mum, Elsie, loved dancing, and was very petite and attractive: Dad tells me that she was often mistaken for his sister! I remember 'Bedford Nana' being well dressed, meticulous about her looks and working in 'top-end' ladies' fashion shops in Bedford. Dad told me though that she also worked in the Cadena Cafe in the Arcade, Bedford. Apparently, Bedford Grandad, assisted by Dad, would occasionally drive the Cadena van to deliver cakes to their shop in town. Later on, Dad would have his own van as part of his Oakley's Carriers business in the 1970s.

In 1937, Dad's younger brother, Brian, was born in Clacton-on-Sea. Although Brian didn't share Dad's passion for cricket, he became a very successful butcher and a well-loved publican in Rushden. He was always joking, with a larger-than-life personality. He won numerous awards for lawn bowls and enjoyed the occasional flutter: an apt word, bearing in mind his interest was in racing pigeons. Brian had two sons: my cousins Simon and Peter.

School

Dad moved to Bedford in 1939 and joined Goldington Road Nursery School, which was close to his home in Irwin Road.

Dad was known as 'Boxer Oakley' during his time at Goldington Road School because occasionally he'd have a playground 'scrap'. I have always known Dad to be very mild-natured: in his later cricket-playing years, however, he would sometimes perhaps become a little frustrated if he wasn't brought on to bowl early enough!

Brian looked up to his older brother and would follow Dad, cycling to Thurleigh at the weekends to see the planes landing during World War II. The sky would be a concoction of smoke and colour: shocking scarlet-red flares from a plane, indicating that there were injured people aboard; or splashes of brilliant emerald-green flares, signalling that everything was apparently in order. The red flare planes were given priority to land over the others. Dad tells me that it was exciting to see, especially during 'Double Summertime', when the local farmers worked well into the evening to get the crops in. Dad and Brian would imagine the stories of those heroic pilots and their adventures in the sky: they were indeed 'game changers'. Subsequently, as a leader in cricket, Dad would need to inspire his team with the confidence to get those vital runs: 'We can do this . . . just need to bowl tidily, or bat sensibly!'

On Sunday afternoons, Dad and Brian would attend Sunday school at Christ Church in Denmark Street. They would be given a Christian text along with the Bible. It felt like an important responsibility, similar to ensuring those match postcards were issued in advance to the 1st XI ahead of Bedford Town's games – usually by the late Ray

Stokes, who was a very accomplished, efficient, and effective club secretary.

Dad enjoyed playing football in the U10 team and was inspired by Mr Crisp, the PE Teacher, who would take the boys training in Russell Park. Dad tells me he played inside right, with number eight on his back: the same number on my shirt when I was at primary school, pretending to be Mick Channon!

Dad's footballing hero was the great Raich Carter, the Derby, Sunderland, and Hull legend who also played as an inside forward and would go on to play for England. Interestingly, he also played for Derbyshire County Cricket Club in 1944. Dad played football throughout his schooling at Goldington Road and he excelled at it. It wasn't until he moved to the Harpur Central School in 1945 (1945-49) that he developed his real interest in cricket.

Social links

Dad enjoyed his paper round at House Newsagent's in Wendover Drive. He got into the discipline of getting out of bed early and getting down to the newsagent's for 6.30 every morning, often hearing our planes on their way out and hoping that they would all return successfully; demonstrating a level of optimism that has followed him since throughout his life. Already he was developing friendships, building his character, and maintaining a strong work ethic – all positive habits that would serve him well.

In Russell Park, Dad met up with the likes of Fred De-Gras, Digger Jones, Arthur Hyams, and Pat Godfrey. They would play 'Americans versus the Japanese', using make-believe weapons, within the 'valley' area of the park. The rolling nature of the landscape, combined with trees and foliage (good for hiding), provided excellent vantage points from which to carry out battles and Pearl Harbor-type attacks. Dad would typically be on the Allies' side and enjoyed allocating responsibilities, just as he would arrange his field positions when he came on to bowl.

A lot of Dad's early friendships involved London evacuees who had been sent to live in Bedford during the War. The majority of them went to John Bunyan School in Castle Lane, close to the town centre. Dad was naturally gregarious and sociable, even from a young age, and had the ability to mix with characters from every social background: he simply just 'got on' with people. Later on, as Bedford Town's skipper, Dad would need the 'dressing room' behind him, usually helped by him winning the toss at the start of play!

Dad says that over the years, in the numerous Bedford Town XIs that he has played for, the dressing room would include doctors, teachers, bank managers, builders, policemen, farmers, architects, entrepreneurs, solicitors, accountants, taxi drivers, councillors, a future mayor, students eager to learn, and last but not least, a milkman. It was a broad spectrum of useful contacts and an impressive supporting network for him to tap into.

During the terrible winter of 1947-8, the rain turned into heavy snow and when it thawed, the Great Ouse spilled its banks well beyond its natural flood plain, over the Embankment and across Newnham Avenue, towards Goldington Road. Dad has vivid memories of seeing displaced fish 'flopping around erratically' across the allotment area, up to Barkers Lane. Dad describes this striking image as unforgettable and as memorable as one of his subsequent three 'nine-fer' match-winning bowling performances, except Dad never felt like a fish out of water at the crease.

During that winter, Dad was determined never to let anyone down and to deliver their newspapers despite the terrible flooding, much to the gratitude of the newsagent,

Mr House. It was a display of defiance and persistent courage similar to that demanded by Mike Rawlinson in order to 'keep an end up' during a limited overs game – to use up the overs and keep the runs down.

Inspirations

At Dad's new school, ex-professional sportsman Claude Knight led cricket sessions with the boys at the Fairfield site on the corner of Shakespeare Road. Dad participated, enjoying the sessions and realising that he was 'quite' good.

With his newfound aptitude for the game, Dad was motivated to learn more, and started getting really keen on playing. He would go down to Newnham Avenue, where Bedford Town were then playing, well before their move to Goldington Bury, to help with the scoring.

Over a couple of seasons, Dad would take his boots and own kit and if Bedford were a man short, he would get the occasional game.

At the time, there was a Bedford Town player called Ken McCanlis, who was a first-class umpire. Ken came from an impressive cricketing family and he felt that Dad looked very promising: he could see real potential; that Dad had the ability to bowl and could be 'an effective away swinger'. Ken asked Dad whether he would be interested in attending a trial at Lord's, so in January 1950, Dad attended a trial at NW8, the home of English cricket, and the rest, as they say, is history.

One of Dad's school friends at Harpur Central School, Carl Hargreaves, also had an interest in cricket and his father, Cyril (who subsequently became the Chief Librarian at Bedford Library), would take the boys down to Newnham Avenue for bowling practice during the week. Cyril was a successful player for Bedford Thursday (businesses closed early on a Thursday) and encouraged Dad to develop his grip of the ball – one finger down each side of the seam, with the thumb in line with the seam underneath.

Dad was good at technical drawing, but he could not quite match the precision of Old Bedford Modernian Peter 'Spike' Findley's detailed, polychromatic scoring in the 1970s/80s. Spike was Bedford Town's equivalent of the late, great Bill Frindall. Another Bedford scorer was Gary Woods: he and others were the unsung heroes, rarely mentioned in the local press coverage, but without them detailed records wouldn't exist and for some players, an insatiable appetite existed for knowing their updated season's averages!

Spike eventually helped out with the scoring for the County, following in the footsteps of people such as the great Tony Pearce. Dad recalls that Spike did a lot for the club on the administration side and was truly dedicated to safeguarding the interests and assets of the club. He remembers the white wooden sign just inside the window as you walked into the pavilion that stated simply in black lettering: 'No spikes allowed in the clubhouse', commenting that the 's' at the end of *spikes* had been crossed through: someone obviously thought that they had a sense of humour! Banter and good humour were never far away.

Dad also excelled at woodwork, learning from an eccentric but highly skilled teacher called Mr Shadrake. This teacher was determined to pass on his talent to his pupils and similarly, many years later, Dad would become more involved in coaching, thereby passing on his own cricketing experience and legacy. Dad also enjoyed his geography lessons with Miss Tysoe, who lived in a cottage by the Fairfield site. He tells me that he was usually in the top five for results at school but alas he rarely entered the top five in the batting order in his ensuing Bedford Town career.

8

Dad recalls that Harpur Central was a rugby school, but his preference had always been football. So, outside of school, Dad would go to the Granada Cinema during the Saturday morning matinee (referred to as 'threepenny rush') and, over time, skippered both their boys' football and cricket teams, called the Bedford Grenadiers. They played in the local leagues, became hotbeds of raw talent and enjoyed loads of sporting success. Dad fondly remembers Kenneth Kerr, a teacher at Rushmore School, who dedicated his time to organising and running the Bedford Grenadiers. Due to Dad's success and growing reputation, he was granted free access to the films and use of the Granada offices if he needed to have a team meeting: clearly, he was well respected, even in his teens.

Leaving School

Dad left school in the summer of 1949, aged just fifteen. In September that year he started at Bedford Battery, Wellington Street, Bedford, which is still on the same site today. He got the job thanks to a social connection: Bedford Grandad had known the owners, the Ayres family, through his work on vehicles and had managed to gain a commitment for Dad to be given a job.

Pete Wadner mentored Dad as he worked in the shop behind the counter. Dad still maintains a high level of respect for Pete, who modelled the right behaviours: whether it was simply making up car plates or carrying out more complex tasks, he did it diligently and thoroughly. Those traits were very important to Dad.

Dad is grateful for his time at Bedford Battery, who were understanding and supportive employers. Over the following few years they allowed Dad to join the Lord's Ground staff during the cricket season (April to September) and to return to them during the autumn and winter months. They were proud that he worked for them and he always looked forward to returning in between his cricketing exploits. It's interesting to make parallels between Bedford Battery, which still exists due to earning a tremendous reputation over the years, and Dad's reputation as a reliable team player, often first to arrive at Bedford Town CC and the last to leave, dedicated in his desire to 'do his best'.

So, even during those impressionable early years, as his talent was just beginning to form, Dad made the most of his expanding social connections.

Lord's Ground staff (1950s)

Cricket Trial

In January 1950, Dad was driven down to Lord's in St John's Wood, London, by Bedford Grandad and Nana: he's certain that this was the only time they saw him with a bat in his hand throughout his career!

In the meantime, Dad's brother, Brian, started a butchery apprenticeship with Mr Tye at the Co-op butcher's in Castle Road. He subsequently joined the Army Catering Corps.

Ken McCanlis had invited to Lords, another exceptionally talented young fast bowler to try out: Bedfordshire-based Hitchin CC player Trevor Morley. He and Dad became good friends.

Still only fifteen years old, Dad felt quite nervous on arrival at Lord's, and he had a few butterflies in his tummy. However, he was also relishing the opportunity to demonstrate his talent. Many years on, whenever I have gone to watch a game at Lord's with Dad, and we've walked down from St. John's Wood Station, through the North Gate entrance and into the Nursery Ground towards the back of the Compton Stand, he gets a tingle, as if he's fifteen again.

Dad remembers practising in the original indoor nets, beyond the Grace Gates and just behind the pavilion. Simple matting was laid down on a concrete base and all the candidates were then called up to bat, and to bowl at each other.

Trevor was quite pacey, but Dad 'got in line', commenting that no helmets were available in those days, nor bowling machines, so every ball had to be treated on its merit. During his life, when the occasional metaphoric

11

short ball would come right at Dad, he simply rocked back, watched it go past his nose and 'got back in line'.

Dad assumed he had been invited to Lord's because of his confident bowling skills: however, he was selected on a regular basis to open the batting for the Ground staff. Many years later, this would help Bedford Town CC 'bolster up' the middle order, usually when a 'collapse' beckoned!

Dad initially stayed at number 350 Edgware Road, owned by a connection of a business contact of Bedford Grandad's. After a month, he found some new, more convenient digs with Alec and Hazel Gull.

Alec was the assistant head groundsman at Lord's. The couple had no children of their own and they really warmed to Dad.

The couple had a spare bedroom in their house, which was situated in the Nursery End, so Dad had the shortest of walks to the daily training sessions. Some of the other candidates had to travel a fair distance every day: so typical of Dad, to land on his feet.

Alec and Hazel (in the 1960s/70s my brother Stephen and I would refer to them affectionately as Uncle Alec and Aunty Hazel) would transport Dad and other ground staff colleagues to various London clubs to play in Sunday fixtures.

Dad recalls playing at the Selfridge's ground in Wembley, at Mortlake CC, and even travelling back to Bedfordshire to play a one-off game at Southill Park; a team that Bedford Town CC would subsequently play in the Beds. County League and where, more than fifty years later, Dad would play his last full game.

Apart from a dose of food-poisoning following a 'dodgy' curry, Dad was lucky and didn't suffer any injuries throughout his ground staff time. However, Dad's constant sciatica problems when playing for Bedford

Town CC meant that he was occasionally unable to release the first ball he bowled at the weekend, resulting in a cry of 'b---er me' – much to the amusement of his playing colleagues. Also, over the years, the top part of his right index finger gradually pointed more towards 'three o'clock'; the result of constantly wrapping that finger around the seam to gain better purchase and off-spin.

The list of talent within Dad's peer group at Lord's is simply staggering. Indeed, it's a who's who of wonderful players who went on to bigger things: a number playing first-class county cricket, some playing for their country, and not just at cricket.

Ray Swallow, for whom Alec and Hazel often provided a lift with Dad on Sundays, went on to play for Arsenal, then Derby County, and for Derbyshire at cricket.

Jim Standen played for Worcestershire, and was an integral member of their 1964 side when they won the County Championship, with Jim topping the first-class bowling averages that year. He also played in goal for Arsenal, Luton Town, and West Ham. Jim also won the FA Cup and European Cup Winners' Cup with the Hammers.

AW (Tony) Catt, whom Dad fondly remembers as being a representative for Sharps Toffees, went on to keep wicket for Kent, where Sharps were based. Tony would emigrate to South Africa and Dad has met up with him there.

Another lifelong friend was Bob Caple, who played for Hampshire, a formidable team at the time. He also played for Middlesex. Bob and his wife Jenny remain good friends. Dad and Bob would go on to work together at Bedford School for many years, until Bob returned to his beloved South Africa. Dad would then travel to South Africa to meet up with them.

The late JT (John) Murray became wicket keeper for Middlesex and England. In 2014, celebrating Middlesex's 150th Anniversary, JT Murray spoke at the luncheon event, saying that he had arrived at the North Gate on the same day in 1950 as Dad. They'd met up with another ground staff member, Brian Hall (who became great friends with Dad), and they were promptly given a broom each to sweep out the Compton and Edrich Stands. He added: 'They were the best days of my life.'

Eric Russell opened the batting for Middlesex and England, and Dad remembers him as a prolific run-scorer.

Don Ward was an exceptionally talented off-spinner who went on to play for Glamorgan.

And let's not forget Trevor Morley, who went on to open the bowling attack for Bedfordshire CCC on a regular basis, and who also played for Hertfordshire CCC. Highly regarded by some top Cambridgeshire cricket clubs, including Wisbech, Trevor sadly passed away in 2013, aged 80 and, like Dad, enjoyed working on his club ground in retirement – perhaps another wonderful testimony to their ground staff days?

The list of names is impressive: to think that these fifteen-year-olds were brought together at the same time, demonstrating an array of sporting talents beyond cricket, is simply astonishing.

Brigadier

The retired Brigadier Lysaght-Griffin paid Dad 'sixpence' a run and 'two bob' a wicket in matches.

Dapperly dressed, complete with bowler hat and brolly, the Brigadier became President of the Lord's Nippers (Sunday XI). He had been an MCC member for many years and motivated Dad's peer group by incentivising the lads. In the nets, he would place half a crown on the stumps, encouraging the boys to protect their wickets.

Mike Neighbour was another of Dad's peer group, who would go on to become Dad's best man at his wedding. He played for St. Giles CC, Cambridge, and enjoyed playing cards, though he would typically lose his money and then try to tap up the Brigadier for a 'sub'.

On the other hand, Eric Russell scored a stack of runs and legitimately got more out of the Brigadier.

The kind-hearted, generous Brigadier would occasionally collect Mum from Euston Station and stop at the famous Leonidas Chocolatiers on Baker Street before dropping her off at Lord's!

Sadly, the Sandhurst-educated Brigadier passed away in 1979, after a good innings of 85 years. He left his mark, however, encouraging and inspiring others, as he had done in the Military many years before while serving in Iraq, for which he was awarded an OBE.

Dad went to Brighton in 1979 for business purposes and thought that he would call in to the Brigadier's last known address, in Brunswick Square, Hove. The Brigadier answered the door, but didn't recognise Dad at first, bearing in mind it had been some twenty-five years since they had last seen each other. 'Then the penny dropped,' like the coin falling off the stumps in the nets at Lord's, and the Brigadier smiled. It must have been quite moving for Dad although another trait of Dad's is that he doesn't show his emotions openly. However, there was the briefest pause as we talked, as Dad reflected on the true gentleman who had helped so many people.

While on the Lord's Ground staff, Dad joined the Stowe Boys Club, through an introduction from Jonny Cox, who lived close by in Paddington. Also known as the 'Pineapple' (after the public house that was converted in 1927), Stowe Boys was financially supported by Stowe School. The club had a formidable local reputation for producing talented young sports people. Some forty years on, in 1992, Dad took the Bedford School U15 XI to Stowe School and remembers the great fun he had at their London-based club all those years earlier!

Dad still keeps in touch with a number of the talented ground staff guys and has enjoyed attending reunions over the years at Lord's.

Dad returned to Lord's in 1951, having passed his driving test in October, which would help him to secure a driving instructor's post during his National Service. He recalls doing some taxi work for Bedford Grandad when he returned from leave. However, that time it was legal and with no cigarette in his mouth!

The MCC was always arranging 'out-matches': representative games against a school or perhaps a club side. Dad remembers the House of Lords versus the House of Commons fixture in 1955. It was played at the exclusive private members' Hurlingham Club in Fulham, London. Dad had by now qualified as an 'A'-listed groundstaff member and was acting as the Professional, spending the afternoon opening the batting and opening the bowling. They clearly wanted the talented twenty-year-old to take the lead!

Dad recalls regularly bowling to the famous film actor Trevor Howard, who also paid the lads to spend some time practising in the nets at Lord's. The actor had already starred in *Brief Encounter* and *The Third Man*, but Dad was never in awe of him – he was just doing his job, turning his arm over and getting paid for it.

Likewise, the great baritone opera singer Dennis Noble loved his cricket and would enjoy being bowled at by Dad and his colleagues.

However, one of the most famous MCC members was the Duke of Edinburgh. He clearly enjoyed his cricket, having previously captained his Gordonstoun School team. Dad recalls, with a smile on his face, an occasion in the early 1950s when the Duke had arrived in a chauffeur-driven car at the nets and stepped out of the car already padded up, to the amusement of the ground staff. One of the nets would be roped off and reserved for the Duke. Apparently, he was very generous to the ground staff: the majority of members paid 'half a crown' or 'two bob', but the Duke paid by cheque, leaving us to assume that it wasn't drawn on the joint account!

In 1955, Dad was invited to play for Bedfordshire CCC against the RAF at Wardown Park, Luton, to enable the selectors to 'have a look at him'. His ground staff colleague JT Murray was playing for the RAF, alongside Doc (Don) Heaton, another good friend of Dad's, who subsequently played for Bedford Town CC.

Western Schools' week

A memorable event took place during Dad's final year on the ground staff. Dad has vivid memories of that incident and although Dad smiles, I sense an internal regret and perhaps a little blemish on his time on the ground staff.

There was a national rail strike in 1955 and as Dad was the only one of the four players selected to hold a driving licence, the MCC gave Dad special permission to sign for a brand-new black Ford Consul at Marble Arch, hired to get the players down to the West Country.

The other three players included the brilliant Eric Russell, and Ronnie Bell, an excellent slow left arm spinner, who would go on to play for Middlesex and Sussex. Dad tells me that Ronnie was also a talented footballer and on Chelsea's books. Dave Widows was the other player, who was 'quite a character' and would eventually emigrate to Australia.

The four young men were to play in a prestigious week of cricket in the beautiful grounds of Monkton Combe School, with its thatched-roof pavilion, and at Downside School. Both schools were close to Bath. They would be based at the stunning Limpley Stoke Hotel, enjoying views over the spectacular Limpley Stoke Valley, also in the Bath area.

They all contributed during the busy week with bat and ball, and acted as good ambassadors, representing the MCC well.

However, on the return trip, Dave wanted to stop at a shop that they had just driven past to buy some sweets for the long car ride back. Dad decided to reverse, as it would have been difficult to turn around. Unfortunately, he hit a low wall outside of the shop, which was out of his vision.

Dad reflected on the minor damage that he was responsible for: having driven carefully throughout the week and having successfully navigated some very narrow country roads, he had broken the rear light on the way back, for a ridiculous reason.

When they arrived in London, the MCC wasn't impressed: in Dad's words, 'the incident didn't go down particularly well'. When the car was later returned, the MCC lost its deposit.

The timing wasn't great, given it was Dad's final year and the MCC was no doubt able to influence outcomes. Dad had taken responsibility for his actions, like he always would do. There would be other times in the future, just occasionally as a skipper, when he would win the toss and make a decision that would prove to be the wrong one. However, on those rare occasions, he just accepted the result and looked forward to the next game.

Army
At the age of eighteen, Dad joined the Army. Bedford Grandad had written to the War Office to try to get a deferment due to Dad's 'professional cricketer' status. They granted him one extra season, so instead of having to join up in April 1952, Dad joined up in December of that

year. His father had just demonstrated another lesson in life for Dad: 'If you don't ask you don't get'.

Dad went up to Oswestry to be kitted out and was then posted to Rhyl in North Wales, with the 31st TR Royal Artillery Regiment.

Dad got on well with Sargent Harris, the RSM, but the CO, Colonel Lyon, was an MCC member, so Dad had an instant connection and 'couldn't do much wrong!'

He remembers playing for the Western Command Army XI: typically, the team was made up of higher-ranking individuals, including officers, but Dad was just pleased to be part of the team, enjoying the sport he loved. This passion for the game and simply wanting to be *part of the team* would never leave him. This is a lesson in life that I have always respected. Although I know that Dad believes that time spent in the Services, despite being enjoyable and playing several cricket games for the Army, probably hindered his progress into the professional cricket arena.

Dad recalls Ray Carter at Rhyl: a Brummie, he was very tall 'quickie' who subsequently opened the bowling for Warwickshire for many years. He was a useful player to have in your side, who could put batsmen under real pressure with his speed. However, he would eventually turn to bowling off-breaks for the County – perhaps influenced by Dad?

Then there was Georgy Moore, who played for Yorkshire 2nd XI. Dad remembers speaking to Geoff Boycott in 1964, when they played at the Goldington Bury, who confirmed that he knew Georgy very well and had played a number of games alongside the ex-Army colleague, in the Yorkshire 2nd XI.

Another player Dad remembers fondly was Wilf Threlfall, a very talented cricketer and footballer who played for Haslington. Wilf's father had played for

Birmingham, Sunderland and Bournemouth. In the 1970s, when Dad had his own van, he called on Wilf, whose daughter answered the door (she was spitting image of her father) and told him that Wilf was unfortunately working down in London with his boiler servicing business. Dad subsequently spoke to Wilf on the telephone, and they reminisced for ages. Wilf had three daughters; Dad had three sons, and they clearly had become great friends when in the Army.

In 1953, Dad represented his Regional Team in a 'three-a-side' National Competition held at Colwyn Bay CC. Basically, two players served as the bowlers and one acted as the wicket-keeper. Other sides then batted and made up the fielding positions. Dad, Georgy and Wilf comprised their selected team. Apparently, they were beating all of the opposition, playing really well as a team and supporting each other, but were brought down to earth by the Birkenhead Park Team in the semi-finals. However, the Army lads did themselves proud and it brought the three friends even closer together.

Dad became a Lance Bombardier: a single stripe, earned as a result of his instructor role. He trained others to drive carefully and took great pride in being able to develop others. In due course, his coaching skills would come to the fore, encouraging Bedford School pupils in the nets, to adjust their grip, stance or bat lift, or to 'reach up and look over that shoulder'.

Chance meeting

In December 1954, Dad came out of the Army and began driving for Bedford Grandad, returning to Lord's in April 1955 for the last time.

Dad's first car was a Singer: nothing to do with sewing machines, but more a collection of car parts that had been put together by his father!

New Year's Eve 1954 proved to be an eventful and fateful evening for Dad. Every Saturday and Thursday evening he would go to Cardington Camp in Shortstown for the music and dancing. They had their own 'All Stars Band', who played all the hits of the day. Occasionally, Dad would have one of Bedford Grandad's cars available to drive to Shortstown; otherwise he would catch the bus from Bedford Market with friends to pick up the free bus travel organised for the return trip home to the Market Square.

Dad enjoyed modern jazz, Miles Davis, Billy Eckstine and Frank Sinatra. He also enjoyed 'big band' music, such as Glen Miller. I remember the Bedford Town CC slip quadrant in the early 1980s, pretending to play trumpets and trombones to *In the Mood*, as Dad came on to bowl!

On *that* evening, mum – 'Dixie' – was waiting for her RAF date to show, but he didn't turn up until later. Dad had already moved in and was dancing with Mum when the chap in the RAF arrived. What followed was not quite *West Side Story*, however: there was a little bit of 'bumping', as Boxer Oakley held on to Mum resolutely!

They married in October 1957. Dad and Mum had their honeymoon in London, arranged by Bedford Grandad. Mum was expecting a West End show, but Dad took her to the Car Show at Earls Court instead. However, they did manage to go to the London Palladium, for a night hosted by Max Bygraves and co-starring the successful Kaye Sisters (interestingly, not actual sisters, but named after their manager), and saw *The Lady and The Tramp* at the cinema. Dad's stand-out memory was the Car Show and his love for cars has never diminished.

Dad really enjoyed working for Grandad in the late 1950s: they used to transport lots of American clients who were working at RAF Chicksands but living in Bedford.

Occasionally, they took American couples to Wimpole Park, Cambridge, which was used as the US Services Maternity Hospital.

Dad managed to negotiate all the alcohol for his wedding reception at the Trades Club in Alexander Road, Bedford, from the Americans. Apparently, it was very strong, close to being pure alcohol. He remembers Grandad getting annoyed because the bar staff gradually became inebriated, and demanding a small refund due to staff members' conduct!

Some of those American clients would carry on sending Christmas cards to Dad long after returning to the States.

Mum had been working in the printing section at Tobler Meltis in Miller Road, Bedford, before moving to Marks and Spencer and then on to Robinson Rentals, on the corner of St. Cuthbert's and St. Peter's Street.

Once Dad had passed his driving test, he would take a 'car-full' of mates to Northampton every Saturday evening to go to Franklin's Gardens, now home of the Saints rugby team. At that time it was a club called The Salon (later becoming Cinderella/Rockafellas). Each friend paid six bob, which more than covered the fuel, or should have done. However, nothing quite prepared Dad for one infamous, eventful Saturday evening.

They were driving back from a good night out and were on the outskirts of Bedford, having just driven over the old Bromham bridge on the A428, when the car ran out of fuel.

Under the driver's seat was a gallon container of petrol in a special compartment: definitely illegal in this day and age of health and safety regulations.

There was no street lighting, so Dad asked Chris Denton to strike a match to enable Dad to see where to pour the petrol. The fumes suddenly ignited, and the explosion blew the canister out of Dad's hands: the car's filler opening was on fire. Dad and Chris shouted to the guys inside the car, as a few of them were asleep after a good night out, to get out of the car quickly, in case it blew up!

Dad singed his eyebrows and burnt the front of his suit, but it could have been a lot worse.

They managed to put some grit (from a roadside store, used for bad weather road coverage) into the tank and put out the fire.

Dad was dreading what his father would say and caught a taxi back to Hurst Grove. The taxi had, coincidentally, been following them back from Northampton, so was just behind them and the driver had witnessed the incident. Dad made a call from a telephone box to speak to his father to forewarn him. Unbelievably, while standing at the phone box, the 'same' car drove past Dad! The remaining lads had managed to start the big old Austin 18, despite the grit in the tank and the fire. It must have resembled a scene from Santa Pod racetrack in Podington.

Chris and Dad still find the incident funny today – that was a 'very' short delivery that Dad needed to deal with!

Interestingly, Dad tells me that a few years later, JT Murray, who was playing for Middlesex by 1952, had been playing Northants in Northampton and he mentioned to Dad that he had seen Bedford Nana dancing the night away in The Salon. Thankfully, he hadn't asked her to dance!

Dad bought a bungalow, Moonglow (named after the song from the film *Picnic*), in Church End, Ravensden, in 1957. Bedford Grandad provided the £300 deposit towards the purchase price of £2,140 and the rest was paid via a mortgage – a colossal £11.74 a month. Those were the days! Bedford Grandad had successfully secured the

Bedford Prison taxi contract at that time and was doing quite nicely for himself.

Dad recalls that Eric Rigby built the bungalow, which was one of a pair. Eric was a friend of Bedford Grandad's. He had married Joan, who was a hairdresser at Brenda's hair salon, where Mum and Bedford Nana had their hair done, situated just above Goldings Ironmongers on High Street. Coincidentally, Brenda was Mum and Dad's next-door neighbour, no doubt handy for the occasional trim.

Moonglow was also only a short distance from Church Lane, which enabled access directly into Goldington and alongside the Goldington Bury, which means so much to Dad, and to which Bedford Town CC moved (from the Newnham Avenue site) in 1956.

Dad remembers the Horse and Jockey pub in Ravensden, which was less than fifty yards from home and owned by two sisters. It was high on the hill and open to the elements, so when the wind really blew, sudden gusts would send smoke pouring down the chimney stack, smoking them out. The locals found it very funny and the sisters would continue to pop down to the cellar to get bottles of light ale while a dense fog engulfed their lounge.

Viv Pell lived in one of the cottages next-door to Dad. Part of the local Pell dynasty, they were a renowned farming family. Subsequently, Pell family members would play at Bedford Town CC.

Wilden was close by, where the great (but short) Bill Peet lived, who would be another Bedford Town CC player. He taught me footballing skills on Goldington Green and was quite a character.

Dad recalls that Derek Hammond, who worked at W H Allen, was the main groundsman (as well as helping with umpiring) at the new Goldington Bury site and lived close by on Church Lane. Bill Peet also helped out with groundsman duties on a regular basis. Bill was a landscape gardener, who would be subsequently supported by his son, Donald, and, in due course, by Norman Cooley. Subsequently, Norman and Dad would go on to take up the player/groundsman role.

Dad remembers Bill offering summer work to various players, including Andy Curtis (OBM). Supporting colleagues is a recurring theme throughout Dad's story: Bedford Town CC became an extension of the players' families.

Dad's first car that he actually bought, as opposed to one of his father's recycling projects, was a grey 'Standard 8' (Coventry-based car manufacturer), purchased in 1958 from Wilson Bros. and Humphreys (who were agents for Standard), on the corner of Cauldwell Street, Bedford.

Dad was still enjoying playing football, playing inside right for Sharnbrook FC, and during the late 1950s the team were a force to be reckoned with, winning a number of league and cup titles.

Bedford Town CC
In 1956, Dad played a few times for the 2nd XI. Skipper Don Andrews was impressed, so Dad stepped up to play for the 1st XI. He enjoyed a good write-up in the local papers at the time: 'Local boy returns from Lord's Ground staff.'

The *Bedfordshire Times* was published weekly on Fridays and gave details of the fixtures and the teams. The *Bedford Record* came out weekly on Tuesdays and had all the results from the weekend, and over the years it made many glowing references to Dad. The word 'veteran' to describe Dad began appearing from the 1970s: I think it was more a term of endearment and a substitute for 'experienced'. I'm positive that it was nothing to do with the wrinkle lines on Dad's forehead, due to his preference for spending a lot of time outside in the elements.

Eric Howard, who worked at Shire Hall in Newnham Avenue, was the 1st XI skipper and a hard-hitting batsman. Eric was younger brother to Jimmy, the renowned Bedford-based entrepreneur (CAEC Howard, originally situated on the St. John's site).

Dad took the place of the retiring off-spinner Fred Sabey and made his mark. Dad had a simple off-break action that would prove very effective over the years. Shane Warne once said: 'Part of the art of bowling spin is to make the batsman think something special is happening when it is not.' Dad was a master of disguise, able to vary his pace, line and length, and to lock into a batsman's weakness like a heat-seeking missile. Over the years, many impatient batsmen would ultimately succumb to Dad's trickery and deception.

The summer of 1957 was fantastically hot. Dad had just got married and had moved into his first home with my mum and had a very good season.

George August was now skipper (father to Pip, who would subsequently become the Town's keeper/captain, and David, who played for the Town) and he was a commanding opening bat, who had also played for the Minor Counties XI in the late 1940s. Pip went on to play for Bedfordshire CCC, and George would eventually become Dad's accountant for his haulage business.

Fred Breeze, who was Dad's bank manager at Barclays in Bedford High Street for many years, opened the bowling with Don Jenkins.

Sid Morris was in the middle order: a strong personality, he was in the local police and sported a striking moustache. He was an Inspector Morse-type character, with an air of authority, and well respected by his team colleagues.

Dad fondly remembers Tom Woolliscroft, who lived on Kimbolton Road with his wife Betty, and who was very dedicated to the club, as a player, as Team Secretary, and subsequently as Club President. He was also Dad's solicitor. As 1960 dawned, the importance of social connections 'came up trumps' again. Tom played a lot of golf with the MD of Sydney Press Ltd, a printing business based in Sydney Road, Bedford, and had mentioned that Dad was looking for a job.

Another wonderful character at the time was Doug Bennett, who skippered the Bedford Ramblers (3rd XI). He had a very successful business on Barker's Lane (Doug Bennett and Sons) and Dad tells me that he was always on call for the local fire brigade.

One fateful evening, Bedford Town CC were holding a selection meeting at Doug's house when Doug's fire station call-out alarm went off and Dad had to quickly move his car out of the way so that Doug could reverse out of his driveway. Thankfully, Doug got to the incident in good time. Doug's son, Terry, would also go on to play for the 2nd XI and knows a number of Dad's cricketing connections. He's also a true gentleman, just like his father was. Terry would become President of the local Pavenham and Felmersham Cricket Club.

Jack Nightingale basically ran the club in the 1950s, and always had a cigarette in his mouth. Joan Brown managed the bar and it was she, along with Betty Woolliscroft, who encouraged Mum to join the Bedford Town Cricket Club Social Committee. Joan's son, John, was a left-hand bat, played for the club and also dedicated lots of time to help with the organisation and upkeep of the club.

Peter and Jean Green also devoted a substantial amount of time in running the club as it evolved during the 1960s and 1970s. They lived on the Embankment, overlooking the suspension bridge. They had a fish round and were instrumental in helping to provide the food for theme nights, such as fish suppers, at the club. Their son Mike would later become President and Chairman of Bedford Town CC.

All these people put themselves out for the good of the club and contributed so much to its development.

Dad was interviewed in early 1960 for the Sydney Press job. He was excited and was looking forward to the challenge, but had an ability to calm his nerves, as if he were about to embark on another long, successful spell from the pavilion end.

Goldington Bury (1960s)

<u>Sydney Press Ltd.</u>
Following Tom Woolliscroft's introduction (Tom would become Mayor of Bedford in 1966), Dad felt he had come across well at the interview and started work there in June 1960.

Dad became a folding machine operator and worked alongside Dave Conway. Dad learnt loads from Dave, and recalls that he had a real 'cor blimey' London accent, even though he lived in Queens Drive. In hindsight, he suspects that Dave may have been one of the London evacuees who had stayed on in Bedford.

Dad really enjoyed his time with Sydney Press and in due course was trained to operate the perfect binder machine. The girls in the team would 'drop the sections' into the machine and, as the sections went around, the spine was cut, glued and finally clamped.

Great, glossy magazines were produced there, such as *Yachting Monthly*, *Good Photography*, *8mm*, and *The Director*: Dad and the team could sneak the first view of each of the publications!

Unfortunately, the pension scheme was part of the infamous British Printing Corporation, so sadly Dad's thirteen years of pension contributions dwindled to nothing once Robert Maxwell had plundered the funds: it was the equivalent of an early scam that plagues the current world we live in!

Dad played cricket and football for Sydney Press, which he really enjoyed. The company was very family-orientated and put on wonderful Christmas parties for their employees' children. Stephen and I would really look forward to those occasions over the years.

One eventful day, Dad was playing in a Bertie Joel '45-over' afternoon cricket game for Bedford Town CC. He went into work in the morning, clocked in, but didn't clock out then went home for lunch and played in the afternoon.

While Dad was playing, he could see Derek Brookes, one of the Sydney Press managers, standing on one of the horizontal slats on the big, white wooden Church Lane entrance gate. What made it worse was that Dad was fielding on the leg side, close to the gate!

Next morning, when Dad arrived at work, Derek demanded that Dad come into his office at 9am.

Derek confirmed that he had given himself a sleepless night in deliberation of what to do with Dad. He explained that he had considered three options: sack him on the spot; ban his overtime for a week; or send him home immediately, where he would have to wait to be contacted.

Thankfully, as with other difficult situations during his lifetime, Dad 'got away with it' and was banned from earning overtime for a week. The lesson, however, was learned.

Dad stayed with Sydney Press until 1974, when he saw an opportunity to set up his own haulage business. He discussed the idea with his boss, Frank Lee, as Sydney Press continued to outsource to transport companies for distribution purposes. Perhaps, Dad suggested, he could provide part of their transport needs?

Cars

In 1962, the year that Stephen was born, Dad was driving a green Minivan. It had a roof lining at the front only; the back wasn't protected, so occasionally my brother would have a few raindrops fall on to him, a similar technique probably used in Guantanamo Bay!

The Minivan was traded in for a four-door Vauxhall Wyvern from Ravensden Crossroads Garage. Dad subsequently found out that the car was rotten underneath and promptly returned to the garage, where he traded it in for a gleaming red VW Beetle. Dad tells me that this was the car in which I was very nearly born in May 1964.

After the Beetle, Dad had the sophisticated two-tone grey MG Magnet, which he cherished, with its dark-red padded upholstery. It had real presence and you felt like you had been born into the aristocracy when travelling with Dad in it!

From 1967 to 1970, Dad owned the Vauxhall VX 490: white with a blue stripe along the sides. He recalls taking us down to Cornwall to stop at Mr and Mrs Verco's bed-and-breakfast hotel in Indian Queens. Dad made a short trip there to visit Peter Richards at his garage close by (Richards and Osborne hauliers). Peter had been a driving instructor in the Army with Dad in Rhyl, and they had remained good friends. Dad remembers Peter fondly and still gets Christmas cards from Ann, Peter's wife, who is a retired local magistrate.

Dad recalls that he hid his cricket kit under the suitcase in the boot, out of Mum's sight, and managed to play a game for the 'drivers' (Peter Richards had a fleet of lorries) versus 'the quarrymen'. While in Cornwall, Dad and Mum were asked by Peter (who was a respected employer and local celebrity) to judge a fancy-dress parade at the town's carnival. Peter also took Mum and Dad to Bodmin Prison: not because they had done anything wrong, but because it had been turned into a nightclub, and a great party was had by all!

Bedford Town CC

Dad skippered throughout 1966-70. The Club was developing a fantastic social culture. The annual ball at the Corn Exchange, which would feature a big swing band, was always sold out. Bedford Town Cricket Club would invite the Bedford Rugby Club members, who would reciprocate when planning their own events. In the earlier years, Joan Brown organised the ball, and then Mum took over for fifteen years.

Andy Curtis would bring his wind-up record player in from time to time and play a selection of vinyl hits of the day, which always went down well.

The enjoyable annual club dinners moved from the Bridge Hotel, just over Town Bridge, to the Bedford Club in De Parys Avenue and they were very well supported. There was a guest speaker after dinner and players could enjoy frames of snooker too, while plenty of drink flowed.

Over the years, the guest speakers included some brilliant cricketers. The great Harry Stillman was usually the organiser throughout the 80s and 90s. Although he didn't play, his larger-than-life personality stood out. He was a great listener too – usually over a pint or two – and was simply a warm, genuine person.

Dad remembers Keith Andrew, who was a fine wicket keeper for Northants and England, speaking at one of the club dinners. He was someone Dad clearly respected: he went on to coach, and write books on the subject, and Dad had played in a benefit game for him.

The list of entertaining speakers who appeared over the decades includes: David English; the one and only Dickie Bird; the humorous David 'Bumble' Lloyd; the sharp-witted Alan 'Lamby' Lamb (twice); the dry-witted Geoff Miller; the joker Graeme Fowler; the legendary Sir Freddie Trueman; Mickey Stewart; Chris Cowdrey; Mike Hendrick; and Geoff Cope, in 1998.

Interestingly, Peter Parfitt was guest speaker in 1991. He had been stationed for his National Service at RAF Henlow, Bedford, until 1958. Peter played for Middlesex, was an excellent left-hand bat and was great friends with

JT Murray, with whom Dad had spent time while on the Lord's Ground staff.

Geoff Millman OBM was playing for Nottinghamshire and got a fixture for Bedfordshire CCC at Trent Bridge. Dad played in the game, but didn't bowl or bat. He remembers, however, that it was the first electronic scoreboard that he had come across. It was the innovative David Hoare who later designed the bicycle wheel of wooden numbers that would form part of the new scoreboard, above the garages, at Bedford Town CC.

In 1963, Geoff Boycott opened the batting with Geoff Millman in the benefit game for Keith Andrews (Northants). Boycott wasn't a Yorkshire 'capped' player at the time: unlike Freddie Trueman, he was classed as a Yorkshire Colt and was given dispensation to play in the game for Bedfordshire CCC against Northants CCC.

The Northants XI was represented by the likes of Colin Milburn and Roger Prideaux – both England cricketers – and David Larter: it was a formidable, mouth-watering line-up.

Dad recalls Geoff Boycott getting 88 in the game, and that Boycott ran out David Hoare on 30. However, it was Geoff Boycott, fielding at long on when Dad was bowling, who called out in his distinctive Yorkshire accent: 'Toss it up Peter, toss it up!' Dad finished with excellent 6-91 figures, though Roger Prideaux hit him a couple of times out of the ground: once into Canvin's garden and then across Church Lane. Boycott's encouragement cost Dad a few runs, but it also proved to be a successful tactic.

Jack Smith, who bowled flat off-cutters, skippered Bedfordshire CCC then. Dad always provided more loop to his bowling, but the similarity in bowling technique meant that it was challenging for Dad to secure a regular place in the county line-up.

33

Dad recalls the touring Australians playing the Minor Counties XI in 1964 at the Goldington Bury, just after I was born. It was the year that Benaud had hung up his national team boots. Bedford Town just had the one player involved: the formidable Bill Chamberlain OBM – and he was 12th man! Dad says that Bill was a strong, imposing batsman who regularly played for the county side.

Dad helped with general ground duties on the day and enjoyed just being part of a spectacle that captured the town's imagination. A temporary stand was hired for the far side of the ground to accommodate the increased number of spectators. Lansdowne Road College students walked around the ground selling match cards. The atmosphere was memorable for Dad and put his beloved Goldington Bury very much on the map.

The Bury House mansion, although derelict, still looked imposing at the pavilion end, its huge striking glass-panelled garden room annex overlooking the outfield. Dad asked whether he could have the ornate weathercock off the roof when the Council finally demolished the building, but on this occasion Dad didn't get what he asked for.

Dad became very good friends with Geoff Millman, who would go on to play for Nottinghamshire CCC and England. Geoff owned Millman Jewellers in Church (Pigeon) Square, Bedford, which is still in existence today. The Millman family lived in a charming converted farmhouse in Felmersham village. Driving over the cattle grid on their long drive towards the house, you were never too sure whether you would be met by a horse, the pet dog, or one of the beautiful Indian peacocks, with their striking iridescent blue colouring, that roamed their land! Although Geoff sadly passed away in 2005, aged seventy, Mum and Beryl remain strong friends.

Then Norman Cooley arrived on the scene, kit bag on his handlebars. He went on to trial with Arsenal, and played for the local Eagles at football. He was a richly talented cricketer, who scored 100s in both innings against Lincolnshire and would eventually become Head Groundsman at Bedford School.

Another good friend of Dad's was the architect Dick White. A tall man, Dick was three days older than Dad, played for Shire Hall before joining Bedford Town CC in the early 1960s, and would open the bowling for many years, demonstrating that wonderful Thomson-style delivery action. Dick and his wife Maggie became good friends of Mum's and Dad's, but sadly both have now passed away; Maggie very recently.

Ray Wood, Dad recalls, had an immaculate, brand-new Ford Corsair (interesting that he remembers the car first!). He was another opening fast bowler and both he and his wife, Pauline, became friends of Mum's and Dad's.

Dad spoke to Ray recently, over Christmas. Reading-based Ray is currently President of the Berkshire Over 60s Cricket XI. Ray's particularly proud of a granddaughter who has been playing representative netball at a high level: probably as proud as Dad is of my own daughter Georgie, who in recent years has played the role of Sandy in the musical *Grease!*

Dad's got great memories of when he was supporting the Bedfordshire U19 XI and they played Berkshire U19 XI at Henlow CC, where Ray was the coach of the visitor's side. Two great friends who had played together years before, having their respective county sides play against each other during the 1990s.

Ted Netherway, who worked at the RAE in Thurleigh and to whom Dad had given the respectable title 'Professor', was a useful slow left-arm bowler. Ted lost his hair in his thirties, while Dad still maintains a full head of hair (for which I'm forever grateful). Ted and his wife Ann also became close social friends of Mum's and Dad's.

In 1965, Dad was awarded the Man of the Match plaque at the Millman Trophy game. Jack Leggat, who was umpiring and had also played the Bedfordshire CCC previously, presented the award.

The game, against Henlow CC at the Goldington Bury, was the occasion of Dad's highest batting score. When Dad had arrived at the wicket, Bedford Town CC were 29-5. Dad was skippering Bedford on the day and took responsibility, hitting 71 in seventy-three minutes.

Malcolm Wynn was in that Bedford Town CC side. He was a very consistent bowler and useful bat, who played for the county. He also supplied us with the occasional television set over the years, from Flitwick. Bluey Thomas was at three, and Julian Dalzell (Old Bedfordian, now living in the USA) was at four. A few years ago, Julian took his US college pupils for a tour around Bedford School and briefly met up with Dad. Pip August was also in the side, as was pipe-smoking Pat Ainsworth.

Dick White and Bob Plowman opened the bowling for the Town, Bob picking up fabulous figures of 2-7. Tony Ingledew, who also went to Harpur Central School and was a couple of school years ahead of Dad, wrapped up a spell of bowling his off-cutters with 4-34. Dad brought himself on to bowl at the death to the tail-enders, picking up 1-0! Henlow, who were chasing 164, were cleaned up cheaply, and Bedford won by a 62-run margin.

And so the social circles, the valuable network of lifetime connections, continued to expand.

Yet another ex-Lord's Ground staff colleague, Brian Hall (who had paired up with JT Murray on 'Day One' back in 1950), was a sales representative for Philips during the 1960s. Brian lived and played for Stanmore CC, and it was Dad who managed to gain the annual Sunday fixture for Bedford Town against Stanmore.

Apparently, Brian was given the nickname 'Float', as kids visiting Lord's assumed that Brian was playing for

Middlesex, not simply on the ground staff, and Brian was overheard saying that he batted at six or seven for the county. His colleagues would politely remind him over the years of his slight exaggeration and the name stuck.

Dad recalls Brian would call into their Ravensden home occasionally and drop off a couple of recently-released 45 vinyl records. If Dad happened to be out completing some taxi work, Brian would be entrusted with the bungalow keys and would pop into to put the kettle on, in readiness for Dad's return!

Dad remembers too the left-hand opening batsman David Hoare, who played for Harpur Sports and Bedford Town CC, and whose son Philip, a talented all-rounder, would go on to skipper Bedfordshire CCC. I remember playing against him in the 1990s, when I was skippering the Sunday 1st XI in the Bedfordshire County League and Philip was captain of a strong Luton Town CC side.

Another star of the Bury ground was the old grey 1950 Ford tractor, supplied by the council for just £50 from Bedford's garage. It had Meccano-style, knee-high horizontal steel bars at the rear, behind the 'bone-shaker' seat, which allowed the gang mowers to be connected. Dad was really fond of that tractor, and apparently saw one recently, in 'good nick', from the same year, fetch £1,400 in an online auction. They've become quite sought-after!

The tractor started on petrol and once it got going, you could switch to paraffin. He even remembers the first three letters of its registration plate: HNM (he seems to have better memory of vehicle registration numbers than he does of family members' dates of birth!). That tractor was a true workhorse for decades and Dad believes that there was nothing more rewarding or satisfying than a freshly 'ganged' outfield. He treated the Bury ground as if it were an extension to his own garden, taking immense pride in its cut, as well as creating those light and dark stripes that wouldn't have looked out of place in the grounds of a

National Heritage site. Appreciated by players and spectators alike, however, such work was probably rather taken for granted.

Propped up against the wall in the cricket club's garage was an aged besom broomstick that Dad would use to remove the tops of the worm casts that would typically appear on the square overnight, when there was moisture about. It looked like one of the magic flying broomsticks used in a game of quidditch from a *Harry Potter* film!

To achieve that ultra-fine cut on the track, the old, trusted petrol-fuelled Suffolk cylinder mower would be brought out from its hiding place in the garage, behind the rusting old wheelbarrow, the white-edged marking-out frame lying balanced across it.

Dad remembers too the heavy, old, russet-coloured solid-steel hand roller, originally kept in the garage. However, over time, it found a home just to the left of the score box, due probably to it being a struggle for people to get it back up the concrete slope into the garage! Unfortunately, Dad points out, the hand roller 'rolled out' of the Bury and vanished one day, never to be seen again! We joke that someone in the Bedford area has a beautifully manicured lawn, perfectly level and ideal for a game of croquet.

The trusty dark-green, heavy-duty Ransomes Mastiff was used to cut the square and latterly served as a replacement roller, once the hand roller had disappeared.

By the end of the 1960s, Dad had moved to Queen Alexandra Road, Goldington. A pair of semi-detached houses had been built on an orchard plot, owned by Laxton Nurseries. The long, narrow garden was full of Cox's apple trees and Conference pear trees, neatly set out. There was also a wonderful weeping willow, with its many drooping branches, similar to the tasselled door curtain used at the Denmark Street chippy to keep the flies out, which sat in the middle of garden. That tree was great for games of hide-and-seek, though you usually got covered in green caterpillars, especially following a mild spring.

Mr Cole, from Wilden, had built the houses. Dad recalls that the builder had a family connection to the actress Maureen O'Hara. Dad was pleased to find out that Tim Machin, another impressive Bedford Town batsman, regular Bedfordshire CCC player and retired Bedford School teacher, is currently living next-door to Dad's old house!

Bluey Thomas built the original front extension, adding a downstairs loo and creating a through-room into the dining room.

Queen Alexandra Road was a tributary off the main A428 Goldington Road and a very short distance from the Bury. A brief walk via King Edward Road and left into Sandy Lane would bring you out opposite Church Lane.

In the late 1960s, Dad would drive every weekend to Roxton to collect the young, big-hitting, talented Wayne Larkins, and I would be sitting in the back of the car. Wayne played one season for Bedford Town CC 1st XI, and played for Bedfordshire CCC before being transferred on to Northants' books: his potential clearly obvious to everyone in the local game.

Also, around this time, the 'quickie' Bill Bushby started playing at Bedford Town CC and went on to play for the county. Bill was a friend of John Brown's, who was skippering at the time. Bill and Di Bushby lived in St Neots, and became good friends of Mum's and Dad's.

The inspiring Pat Briggs arrived at Bedford Town CC from Letchworth CC. He was a teacher and Master in charge of cricket at Bedford School. A consistently top-four batsman, he was very stylish, and played regularly for Bedfordshire CCC.

Dad recalls a wonderful character who arrived on the scene in the late 1960s: Gordon 'Brasso' Brice OBM. Gordon was a local builder/developer for Brice and Dickens, who played for Northants at cricket and centre half for Luton Town, Wolves, Reading, Fulham, and Ayr Utd. He was also a 'scratch' golfer. Gordon built the houses just set back from Shakespeare Road, which were homes for Bedford Prison officers.

Dad was smiling when he told the story of when the club got Gordon to play a 'comeback' game for Bedford Town CC with Dad managing to kit him out with a shirt, flannels and boots. Apparently, Gordon came racing in off a long run-up, assuming that he would be able to bowl his old fast/medium pace from his very first ball, but just before reaching the umpire, he let out a cry of pain and an expletive (that probably wouldn't be referred to in the School song), pulled up with a torn calf muscle in both legs and had to be carried off by his fellow players!

Sadly, Gordon, passed away in 2003, aged seventy-eight. As he got older, he would turn up in his car at the Goldington Bury to watch a game. Dad remembers a day during Gordon's final years: he had managed to walk through the gates at Burnaby Road and sit on the first bench, facing the Bedford School wicket, despite the onset of illness, because he needed to be part of the action. However, he always blamed Dad for talking him into playing again!

'Bluey' Trevor Thomas was a local builder. As well as building the extension at the front of the Queen Alexandra house, he also later installed the VELUX windows into the roof at 46 High Street (the Oakley Farmhouse). Trevor went to Harpur Central School too and was a brilliant Randall-esque cover fielder and a very useful middle-order bat. I remember watching him in the field when I was young; not just walking in as the bowler commenced his run up, but moving swiftly, purposefully, ready to pounce, almost expecting the ball to arrive in the area that he patrolled.

Dad always felt that Bluey probably saved 20/30 runs in the field every game, which could easily translate into the margin of victory. Trevor also went on to play for the County and was another great member of the Bedford Town touring party. Dad also recalls Trevor's mother, Kath, who had a strong personality who was well known at Bedford Rugby Club for her vocal support. She always supported her son and, likewise, Bluey was always encouraging his fellow players, which is so important when facing a long session in the field.

Malcolm Stedman was another 'run machine' throughout his years at Bedford Town CC and playing for the County. Indeed, even during the late 1990s, when I was selecting the Sunday 1st XI and Malcolm was approaching fifty, his name was usually the first on my selection sheet. He was always very composed, a patient batsman who could build a decent score and had the ability to deal with the new ball.

Malcolm was also an excellent hockey player and played for the Bedford Hockey team, who used to share the Bury in the 1970/80s, typically playing from September/October through to March/April. The additional income boosted the club's finances and helped to maximise usage of the Ground outside of the cricket season.

Dad wrapped up the 1960s on a high, taking 9-61 against Huntingdon: on this occasion he didn't take the first nine wickets, so no one would be blamed for Dad not 'cleaning up' the opposition single-handedly! Although Dad remembers that Dick White picked up the remaining wicket and finished up with 1-26! However, that wasn't to be the case during a similar wicket haul in the 1970s.

'Another nine-fer'(1970s)

Teas

During the early 1970s Dad was still working for Sydney Press, and Bedford Town was building its reputation, and not just on the field: the teas were the best for miles. Mum drew up rotas and a number of the wives, including Liz Rawlinson, Sally Cooley, Sally's sister Jean, Beryl Pratt, and Audrey Hoare stepped up to prepare excellent, mouth-watering spreads, as well as lunches for the all-day games.

Not many clubs could boast homemade chocolate Rice Krispies, coconut pyramids and fruit scones among their afternoon cake selection.

If you were batting at the time, or next in, it was very difficult to resist the temptation to nibble. Dad's positive that we probably gained a few fixtures over the years due to the strength of our teas!

We reminisce about the old, large tea urn that sat just inside the kitchen door. Even on beautiful weekend afternoons the players enjoyed their hot tea, using the pale green crockery that littered the kitchen. I remember Andy Curtis OBM, another stylish bat for Bedford, who was my cricket coach and a teacher at Bedford Modern School, referring to 'marginal utility', or extra satisfaction gained, where *your desire for tea actually increases*, during one of his memorable O-level Commerce sessions. I may even have earned an extra mark by using Bedford Town CC as an example!

Dad refers to the rectangular walnut collection box, with its handles dovetailed underneath at both ends, which would be taken around the ground. Dad would ask me to shake it out loudly, to encourage small donations from spectators. The proceeds helped to fund new balls for future games.

The ground was often packed on a sunny afternoon. The Church Lane gate would be open well before the start time, to allow for cars to drive through and secure a pitch around the Goldington Bury ground. There were times when one of the more 'mature' spectators would pull up at 2pm, as play had just commenced, and the players would be giggling as the very slow vehicle drove across the outfield to the deep extra cover position on the far side, usually crushing some of the white boundary boards that had been pushed into the boundary line.

Typically, there would be a huddle of cars in The Spinney corner and also, just in front of Canvin's garden fence. Once they gained their pitch, the folded chairs would be positioned in front of the car, with the bags of humbugs and barley sugars aplenty.

Dad also recalls those constant shouts of 'Sit down!' or 'Hurry up!' as non-cricketing spectators walked in front of the big white sightscreens at each end. It was particularly amusing, though not usually for the batsman facing at the time, when the 'guilty' person actually sat down on the sight screen wheel, not appreciating that sporting a navy-blue blazer, a Sinatra-style trilby and smoking a pipe like Harold Wilson, would be a distraction.

It was traditional for players to walk around the edge of the boundary during the game, in little groups, each taking a cricket ball and competing to see who could roll their ball closest to the boundary marker. Conversations would take place with the spectators and, just occasionally, the player would need to answer the delicate, subtle question put to him: 'Why did you play that shot?'

The players' wives offered tea and cake, which always went down well, and was another way of supplementing the cash float. Occasionally, the kitchen window would be opened on its hinge and refreshments passed directly out to the regulars, who sat under the canopy at the front of the pavilion. The tea ladies did a brilliant job keeping everyone fed and watered, always ready to go the extra mile to help out.

For those ex-Bedford Town cricketers reading this, I want to take you on a brief journey back in time for a couple of minutes. It's a beautiful weekend in early May (last week's game had been washed out!), you're driving from the town direction, past Turner's Post Office (where Mick and Tim Meadows lived with their parents, both OBMs and Bedford Town cricketers) then turning left into Church Lane; opposite the barber's shop on the corner of Sandy Lane, you can just hear the church bells ringing in the background. The expanse of Goldington Green is on your right, and on your immediate left is that block of white flats known as Heron Heights. You drive past the Falstaff on your left and around that sharp left-hand bend at Canvin's white-gated lodge house (famous local butcher family), on the corner. The St Mary's Church bells now ring more loudly as you're welcomed in towards the Bury. You're looking forward to it, you feel younger: will you get some runs, will you get some wickets, and will you bat today? Practising a few strokes in the French windows this morning, you looked in good nick: forget about anxiety, stress, family responsibilities, those little aches and the Monday to Friday 9-5. As you drive through the open iron and mesh gate at the back of the pavilion, St Mary's is now looking down on you – you're going to be all right, you're going to do well, you're going to play your part, you might even get a mention in the *Record*!

Finally, you drive beneath the dark canopy of foliage and branches of those tall horse chestnut trees. You're actually driving on part of the original carriage drive that linked the Lodge House to the Bury House mansion, now covered by a block of flats overlooking the ground. You turn left, alongside the brick-built score box and then out into the sun-filled, blue-sky opening, a beautiful oasis: a freshly 'ganged' outfield awaits; the right-hand dressing room door welcomes you in. You claim your chrome clothes hook. You're in the safe zone. You can be yourself and enjoy the banter; the world is good. You have arrived.

Guillotine Incident

Dad and I recall one famous 'near-miss'. I was up in the score box placing the metal number plates into the narrow slots on the back of the white wooden score board. Each metal plate had a narrow rim at the top, a lip that had been bent square on, designed to prevent it from falling out. One Sunday afternoon, I tried to slot a number representing the batsman at the top of the scoreboard just above David Hoare's wooden numbered cycle wheels. We rarely used the slots higher up, save for prestigious county or cup games. The sharp-edged metal plate fell out of the front of the scoreboard in front of the right-hand garage, possibly a twenty-foot drop! I remember looking through the little square opening with my heart in my mouth. I could see old Judge Berry perched on his pole – he used to spike his pole in the ground and unfold a small leather seat at the top – sitting in front of the garage. Thankfully, the metal plate had fallen on the spot where the grass met the concrete slope into the garage. The Judge was oblivious to the 'blade' that had fallen behind him: however, if it had not been for the slope into the garage, he might have been another four feet back and he would have been guillotined! In future, I would just stick to showing wickets, overs, last man out and fall of last wicket: forget the batsman's number.

I remember that Dad's dark-brown, antiquated leather cricket bag always attracted comments in the dressing room, usually from those sporting huge modern 'coffins' that provided enough space for the kitchen sink. The Brigadier had bought the bag for Dad in 1955 when he left the Lord's Ground staff. Dad says he bought it from the Army and Navy Store in Victoria, London, and had added in some new pieces of kit for him. I remember Dad's old, grey, woollen cricket socks were always in his bag, sometimes with sharp wooden splinters attached to them, if he'd been playing away at somewhere like Eversholt CC, where they had a timber floor in the dressing room. Dad tells me that he put the old, bedraggled bag into his skip only recently, and thankfully the fifty-plus-year-old jock strap went in with it!

A huge regret of Dad's was swapping his navy blue MCC cap for a dark green Aussie 'Baggie' cap. So the story goes: Bedford Town CC were playing an Australian touring team in the 1970s, Australian Old Collegians. It was a midweek fixture, and after the game, Dad reckons, he had a few too many 'light and bitters' and agreed to swap his prized Lord's Ground staff cap for the cheap Aussie version. The baggy green was in fact too big for Dad's head and probably more suitable for busking purposes outside Charing Cross! I believe it was Simon Barnes, the sportswriter, who said that 'the traditional dress of the Australian cricketer is the baggy green cap on the head and the chip on the shoulder!'

In 1973, the late Robin Fletcher, assistant Headmaster of Bedford Preparatory School, organised the enjoyable Harrogate Cricket Tour: more tours would follow, due to its success. On that first tour, Dad shared a room with Norman Cooley and Bob Caple, who came up to Yorkshire to play in a game. Dad described the Adelphi Hotel, now converted into residential accommodation, as a 'bit of a rabbit warren': lots of cramped rooms, with little space to 'swing a Grey Nicholls'.

Bedford Town CC played Harrogate, York, Otley, Craven Gentleman and Idle. Dad recalls being hit for four sixes in an over during the Idle game by a powerful Crawford-White who, Dad understands, went on to play at a higher level. Dad remembers his team colleagues laughing, when a certain Rodney Fensome OBM, exclaimed: 'That's gone all the way to Bradford, Pete!' That particular Bradford League Club had an amazing history itself, with the great Sir Jack Hobbs beginning his illustrious cricketing career there.

On the tour, Dad chatted in the bar after the game at Otley CC and asked the local players whether they knew Georgy Moore, Dad's old cricketing colleague from his Army days. Amazingly, Georgy lived locally and was well known by the players. Dad was able to speak to him and he joined them for drinks in the clubhouse at Otley. Georgy's first words to Dad were that he remembered the 'high left elbow' when Dad was playing forward: he could tell that Dad was a product of Lord's!

Another fantastic fixture for Bedford Town CC was the Cross Arrows game arranged by Pip August, who was working in the Lord's Cricket Office at the time. Cross Arrows CC played on the Lord's Nursery pitch, near where Dad had stayed with Alec and Hazel during the 1950s.

Bedford Town CC took a strong XI down to Lord's, skippered by Mike Rawlinson, and managed to beat the home side with a match-winning knock from the hard-hitting all-rounder, Peter Davison.

The Town continued to dominate the annual local Hospital Cup, played in Bedford Park. The local village and town teams would always try to raise their game against Bedford Town CC, who typically would put out formidable line-ups, including county players. Dad reckons that he has around thirteen winners' trophies.

More latterly, Bedford School connections formed their own Ousels XI, while BMS connections, teachers, parents, current students, and old boys created a Modernians XI. Both these sides would feature Bedford Town CC players and some of the Twenty Over cricket was simply spectacular to watch, and usually very well supported, with talented players who were in the same side at the weekend playing against each other during these midweek Cup battles.

A couple of very useful Bedford West Indian cricketers – Barry Dwyer, a hard-hitting batsman and bowler, and Glen Riley, a very useful 'correct' early order batsman – played for the Town from time to time. During the 1970s, the Bedford West Indian local team was a strong side and were tough opponents for any team drawn against them in the local Cup competitions.

Dad remembers all the jugs of beer that he had to buy over the years, typically for a five-wicket haul. Whenever he ended up with a 4-fer, there were cries of 'jug avoidance' in the dressing room. The banter was always fantastic, emanating from some wonderful personalities. I recall in the late 1980s/early 1990s that Dad had his own chair in the showers, occasionally frequented by Robin Fletcher, which provided an opportunity for him to rest his limbs after a long spell, and to occasionally smoke a cigarette as he reflected on his performance.

Club Game

Bedford Town's annual club game, at the end of the season, was a 'must attend' for all playing members.

Initially, it was played as an under-30s side versus the over-30s. Over the years, this morphed into two mixed sides, including wives, girlfriends, and children of players, who enjoyed a fun-packed, limited-over game. I recall that in the 1970s, Bluey's Jack Russell was also selected!

Typically, the bar would remain open throughout and a mouth-watering spread or a barbecue, using those old oil drums kept behind the pavilion, followed the spectacle.

Chauvinistic players would try to 'crowd the bat', when one of the ladies arrived at the crease. During a normal league game, the batsman would probably make a plea to the umpire that the fielder's shadow was 'on a length', during a sunny afternoon. When realising that the

48

incoming player was, say, Fran Steadman (Malcolm's wife, who had played cricket at the highest level), respect was shown and the field would move back.

Plenty of 'friendly' sledging would take place and the male players were supposed to bat with their wrong hand. This 'handicap' would always meet with laughter, and in the slips you would hear: 'Well, you can't bat with your normal hand, so I think we're safe today!'

The club was always very family-orientated. All of us players' children would typically make our way to the far side of the Bury upon arrival. Jackets or jumpers were laid down as pretend goalposts or we would use the fence as the wicket.

With no mobiles or screens to distract, the children of the players over the years could play the game, participate in hours of exercise and still be able to watch their father 'grab a wicket', take the catch or ping one to the boundary.

We just had to take care not to hit our own ball onto the playing outfield: if you did, you had to wait to the end of the bowler's over to retrieve it or, more often, the nearest player would simply smile and send the ball back towards the cluster of children who would become players in the future.

In 1973, my youngest brother, Jon, was born, and it was during that year that Dad began to see the potential opportunity for setting up his own transport business.

Oakley's Carriers
In 1974, as if he were taking a quick, sneaky single in the last over, Dad grabbed the opportunity to move into the haulage sector, backed by his Sydney Press boss at the time, Frank Lee.

Dad had to sell his beloved yellow Ford Cortina GT to enable him to buy a van. I remember earning decent 'bob-a-job' money washing that particular car at weekends.

However, he remembers, smiling, before he'd owned the Cortina he'd had a red Simca 1301. He'd sold it on to Norman Cooley and, so the story goes, Norman told Dad that Sally (Norman's wife), while out driving one day, went to change gear and the gear lever had snapped off in her hand.

Dad had bought the car from Peter Hooker (Hooker and Roberts, based in The Grove) and over the years had traded a number of cars with Peter. Peter and his wife, Simone, became friends of Mum's and Dad's. Peter was also on the social committee for Bedford Town CC.

So, Dad's treasured Ford Cortina with the black vinyl roof, which had carried the family safely down to Cornwall and back, was traded in for the Commer Van. It had been a security van, with huge solid bumpers, and looked the sort of armoured vehicle you would expect to see in a military conflict zone.

I helped Dad put his white stickers from Goldings onto the Prussian blue sides of the van, remembering to put an apostrophe just before the 's' in Oakley's Carriers. I was impressed that Goldings even had an apostrophe sticker.

Dad kept his union card and stayed connected with Sydney Press while beginning to build his own contacts, such as Diemer Reynolds, Robin Field Press, Stephen Howard Press and Terry Pond. Bedford was a hot-bed of reputable printing-related businesses at the time. Dad's list of introducers continued to grow, often through referrals or recommendations: times were good.

Dad also picked up work with Newnorth in Bedford, a well respected commercial printers, where he dealt with Paul Hooley, another ex-Sydney Press Ltd employee who became Mayor of Bedford in 1978.

Dad also managed to secure a contract with Sterling Safeway Ltd, the London Road foundry, where he dealt with Sid Golder, who got on really well with Dad. The firm made moulding boxes and Dad would deliver them to factories around the Midlands.

On his return trips, Dad would call into the Eastern Gas Board in Leicester, pick up boxes of used listing paper and drop them off at Podington Airfield.

'Nolly' Richard Ebbs OBM was running a sideline wastepaper business from the airfield and agreed a contract with Dad to handle some deliveries. The onward trip would usually be to Peterborough Mill. Nolly played cricket for Biddenham Esquires and was another great ally of Dad's, who recalls that my brother Stephen had a weekend job moving boxes of paper about at the airfield Site. Dad recently spoke to Nolly and he mentioned an ideal title for this book could have been *Spinning Around the World*!

Nolly's older brother, Barry, was also an OBM and played for Bedford Town CC with Dad. Barry worked as an accountant for Rentokil's South African arm and currently lives in Cape Town. He is a member of the famous Newlands Cricket Ground there, which sits in the shadow of the imposing Table Mountain, home to Western Province, and Dad would subsequently visit him there.

Gale connection

During the 1970s, Mum became Ron Gale's secretary. Ronald Gale OBM had been Bedford's mayor in 1955 and 1956 and was a renowned Bedford dignitary. Ron was also Bedford Town's President. Ron, his brother, Horace, and his wife, Marjorie, were very involved with the local Bunyan Baptist Church community and many good causes have benefited from a Gale Family Charity Trust Award over the years.

Ron asked Dad and Mum if they would like to move into the Queens College farmhouse at 46 High Street in Oakley as temporary caretakers, 'rent-free'. Although the house was being renovated, the main jobs had been completed and the property was wonderfully positioned in the village for both the shops and the pub. They grabbed the opportunity and moved into the beautiful farmhouse in 1978.

The house was full of original features: low ceilings, wonderful beams and an inglenook fireplace. It was laid out over three floors and Stephen, Jon and I had the top floor to ourselves. The upstairs floors creaked a lot; rather like Dad's back did when he tried to release the first ball of the season and had not been able to make the previous week's nets session.

Eric Clare, a highly skilled carpenter, continued to work on internal aspects to the farmhouse, and Dad recounts that it was like watching a true master at work – and was handy for the occasional picture that needed mounting!

Ivor Seabrook farmed the land to the rear of the farmhouse, down to Stafford Bridge on the Great Ouse. There was a fantastic orchard adjacent to the farmhouse: apple, pear, and plum trees were plentiful, so we never had to buy any. We would, however, occasionally put a trestle table out the front to offer fallen fruit to the villagers.

Opposite the farmhouse was the village Post Office, run by Denis Canty, whose father, Ted, had worked with Dad previously at Sydney Press.

A couple of houses down from the Post Office, towards the Bedford Arms, local builder Brian Craddock lived with his wife Pam and their children, Gary and Bev.

The Perm
Pam was a hairdresser and talked Dad into having a perm, like a number of famous footballers such as Kevin Keegan (remember the Brut 33 advert?). Dad thought he would get it done in the winter to avoid comments from his cricket colleagues.

The weekend he had the curly hairstyle applied, he wandered into the Balloon Pub in Foster Hill Road – very much the drinking establishment for Bedford sportsmen in the 1970/80s – and as he made his entrance, Bert Potter, the renowned landlord, exclaimed: 'B----- hell, what have we got here?'

I happened to be in the farmhouse kitchen when Dad was given the perm treatment and, as Pam had some perm lotion leftover, I also had it done. When I went to school on the Monday, the hairstyle was met with plenty of amusement and I picked up the temporary nickname of Shirley (Temple) from friends and teachers. I recall Andy Curtis giving me a roll of eyeballs, followed by an 'Oakley Lad'. Just like Dad, though, I didn't have any regrets, and Dad's qualities and personality shone though from beneath the ringlets!

Caterham School Incident

In 1976, John Robinson, master in charge of sports at Bedford Modern Junior School, asked Dad if would drive the school minibus down to Caterham School in Surrey. Dad was self-employed by then, with his own haulage business, so he could be flexible and agreed to help out.

I was playing in the Under-11 cricket side with some young quality players including Alan Fordham, who went on to play for Northants CCC. As we came off the M1, we broke down for the first time. The AA arrived and got us going, but within 30 minutes we had broken down again in Seymour Place, just off Baker Street.

The AA returned to assist, and in the meantime an elegant, well-dressed lady, who had seen us break down and wanted to help, invited us all into her town house. She even took a couple of us to a local shop to get some nibbles in. After a short food break and with the school minibus still being worked on, the cricket players walked down to Hyde Park and played some cricket and football.

Mr Robinson contacted Caterham School and the match had to be cancelled. Dad remembers the day vividly, and although we never reached our intended destination, my team colleagues and I thoroughly enjoyed the day out. We sent the lady a thank-you card, signed by everyone. Dad remained calm and pragmatic through the incident and it's only now that I'm aware that he had to turn off Park Lane and find a safe place to pull up before the vehicle ground to a halt!

In the early 1970s, Mike Rawlinson skippered the Town for a couple of years. Mike was a maths teacher at Bedford School, a northerner, and a gutsy opening bat. Occasionally, he would take his car to away fixtures, and I discovered that his car was the one to avoid for transportation. Mike had a habit of constantly moving his right foot up and down on the accelerator when he spoke (which was often), and he would depress the pedal and take his foot off when he stopped speaking. I remember one Sunday fixture when I had volunteered to help with some scoring; I had noticed that there was room in Mike's car (now I understand why), so I sat behind Mike for the journey to Aylesbury. I promptly threw up when we reached the ground!

Paddy Considine was another great friend of Dad's in the 1970s. Paddy came up from Beckenham CC, having moved to Bedford with his employer, Dudeney and Johnston (grocery chain). He also got mum a job in their costing office.

Paddy played for Bedford Town CC and played for the county in 1971. He was a prolific left-arm spinner who could really turn the ball. A Liverpool-born slow left armer, he went on to skipper Exmouth and play for Devon. Dad recalls Paddy having a fantastic sense of humour. Dad would continue to visit Paddy when he moved down to the South-West. Paddy owned a sports shop in Exeter and Dad would occasionally drop off Gola sportswear when carrying out trips down to the South-West. Paddy took on a snooker club business next, before running a charter boat service off the Exmouth coast. Sadly, he passed away at the age of seventy-seven, but for Dad, his huge personality lives on.

Dad recalls too Bob Plowman, an opening bowler who 'had a great action'. He played for the Town as well as the Igranic, in Kempston, which became Cutler Hammer Europa CC in due course.

Bob Demming was another useful all-rounder in the 1970s. In 1975 Dad would take 9 for 35 at Aylesbury (his second 'nine-fer': and he would achieve three in total over three decades). He took the first nine wickets during the game and instructed Bob to bowl wide, but obviously within the return crease. The batsman unfortunately chased a wide one and Bob picked up the last wicket. It reminds me of a quote from the great English fast bowler Sydney Barnes, commenting on Jim Laker taking all ten wickets for England versus Australia at Old Trafford in 1956: 'No bugger ever got all ten when I was at the other end.'

Bob also played on the wing for Bedford Blues Rugby and was part of the victorious Blues 1975 team that beat Rosslyn Park in the John Player Final, scoring a couple of tries. Dad recalls that it was the great Budge Rodgers' last game for the Blues.

Interestingly, Dad still has the Aylesbury scorecard and he noticed that the charismatic Rob Howarth, my BMS 6th form tutor, opened the bowling that afternoon. Also, alongside Bob, playing in the Centre position at Twickenham was Richard Chadwick, another teacher, who was the master in charge of rugby at BMS. Behind the Bedford Blues winning team was no other than the inspirational coach, great leader and Bedford Town cricketer Pat Briggs.

55

A number of talented Bedford Town cricketers played in the Bedfordshire CCC team that beat Yorkshire 2nd XI on their own patch, up in Barnsley, in 1972. Andy Curtis, Bob Demming, Bill Bushby, and Dad's Lord's Ground staff friend Trevor Morley also played in that memorable game.

Two left-arm 'quickies' joined the Club. Rod Starling was in the police and Dad recalls that Rod would occasionally have to deal with assets that had to be confiscated from the public, which could not be reclaimed. At times this would include vehicles, and Rod suggested to Dad that if he needed to replace the Commer Van, this could be a cost-effective way of finding a replacement! Rod later joined the Hong Kong police force.

Malcolm Glaister was a very tall left-armer, who had previously been on Kent's books. Dad recalls speaking to Tony Catt in South Africa subsequently, who remembered Malcolm playing for the County's second XI.

Table tennis

During the 1970s, Bedford Town CC formed a table tennis team in a lower division of the Bedfordshire Table Tennis League. Dave Hill was very much at the heart of the squad: 'Hilly' was a superb keeper/batsman and another OBM. Dad and I also participated, alongside some great characters including: Mick Meadows OBM, John Powell OBM, Dave Harris OB, Chris Whiting, 'pipe-smoking' Pat Ainsworth, Kevin Atkins, Dermot Walsh and other Town cricketers. The games were played mid-week in the evening and gradually the Bedford Town CC squad grew in numbers. We developed quite a strong local reputation. I particularly remember Dad's back-hand smash, which was usually a winning shot when he got it right.

The table tennis squad won a lower league title and I recall visiting teams would complain about the poor lighting. Furthermore, the ceiling at the Goldington Bury Pavilion was not the highest, so away teams occasionally struggled to play the loop shot. We obviously knew about the issue and adapted our game, so in hindsight, perhaps, we might have had a slight competitive advantage. However, most importantly, the bar would remain open throughout the evening.

Dad fondly remembers Barry Stuart, a larger-than-life, ex-Guardsman: the debonair, wicketkeeper for the Town during the early 1970s. He recalls Barry's constant "Sorry!" as he let another one slip through his webbed gloves, usually to big Dick White. However, as Barry was such a nice, well-regarded guy, no one seemed to mind.

Barry was a representative for Pol Roger Champagne and got Mum a job in his office in South Audley Street in London's Mayfair. Barry happily supplied plenty of champagne for Bedford Town CC socials, so it's not surprising his fellow players tolerated the occasional dropped catch or fumble!

Dad would eventually move Barry back closer to his roots in Barnsley, using his Oakley's Carriers van, during the mid-1970s.

Helping to move his teammates was not uncommon for Dad: he was always willing to put himself out and support a fellow player or friend. Ian McLaren OB was a talented batsman, playing for both Bedford Town CC and the County, who became a brilliant heart surgeon. Dad moved him down to Southampton for work purposes during the 1970s.

Another character who arrived at Bedford Town CC was Geoff Irvine OBM, who had played for Diemer and Reynolds previously. Dad recalls that he used to try to disguise his off breaks and could also hit the ball hard. Big Geoff carried out the extension work for the pavilion to the score box, including extending the dressing rooms.

Geoff would occasionally offer work to club players. Geoff became Chairman of the Bedford Blues Rugby Team and was well respected within the sporting community. Another Blues Rugby Board member was Ian Bullerwell, who was Dad's insurance broker for many years, helping to provide him with the various forms of insurance cover he needed.

Peter Davison, when working on the Covent Garden contract, also offered work to a few of the Bedford cricketers, including Andy Curtis, and was able to offer Dad work with the van. Peter was a true team player, offering temporary work for several Bedford Town CC players over the years, including me and my older brother, Stephen: we both had jobs during the summer holidays thanks to Peter.

Mick Meadows tells me that he remembers taking a Bedford side down to north London to play against South Hampstead for a Sunday 1st XI fixture. They had a rather quick West Indian bowler, Vic Brown, who had a distinctive Malinga-esque round-arm sling action. Dad went into bat and apparently 'shouldered arms', losing his off stump, and was out cheaply. He returned to the pavilion, sat in a chair outside on the grass, calmly lit up a cigarette with his team colleagues and commented: "Well I've never been cleaned up like that before." Peter Davison responded: "I'm not f------ surprised Peter!"

Another bubbly character that Dad fondly remembers was the late Albert Saunders. Albert led the Ramblers XI for many years, which was the perfect side to blood new, young players, as well as accommodating those closer to retirement. Albert wasn't the tallest of cricketers, but he had a fantastic sense of humour and had an infectious laugh that would light up the dressing room.

Dad has great memories of my older brother's 5-fer against Middlesex U15 XI at Eversholt CC, on a lovely summer's afternoon in 1976. The ground had a tree inside the boundary (similar to the famous original tree at Kent's St. Lawrence Ground in Canterbury, which I understand came down in a storm in 2005) and is one of the most picturesque village settings in the county. Interestingly, Philip Hoare was in the same U15 Junior County side. Stephen had a simple but effective slow left arm action and still occasionally puts his flannels on for Olney CC, where he lives with wife Kim and works as an estate agent.

Dad would be by the side of my younger brother Jon, encouraging him to bat well and bowl line and length, during his Bedfordshire County U19 games. He also played in the same game as me, against Bury St. Edmunds CC, when I scored my maiden ton for Bedford Town.

Where cricket and cars were concerned – his real passions – Dad was always there for his sons. Family weekend trips such as the theatre, cinema visits, or the occasional London Museum adventure, were Mum's domain.

In the late 1970s a young lad and a good school friend of my older brother, Richard Mellor, played for the Town. He was an opening bowler with a long run-up. Dad remembers that Richard's parents lived on the other side of Church Lane, opposite the Bury, and would have to occasionally retrieve the cricket ball from their front garden. Richard moved down to Thames Ditton in Surrey. I remember throwing sticks up to knock the conkers down from the higher hanging branches from the tall trees, to the left of the score box, with Nigel, Richard's younger brother.

Mick Meadows recalls Phil Hoare making his debut for Bedford Town 2nd XI as a teenager in the late 1970s. Bedford was put into the field and, so the story goes, without being instructed to do so, Phil walked to the specialist 1st slip position. Rod Fensome, who was keeping that afternoon, politely enquired: "What are you doing there?" Phil replied: "I'm a very good slip fielder."

Dad calmly chipped in: "Well, young man, I'm a very good slip fielder, but I'm older – now f--- off."

Left stranded

Dad has a smile on his face when he recalls the infamous Wembley Cricket Club Dinner in 1970.

Dad was skipper of the Town and had been invited by Peter Wray, the Wembley skipper, to attend their dinner. A good night was had by all, but a couple of Dad's Bedford playing colleagues who had travelled down to the venue in Victoria, London, including Mike Green (now Patron of Bedfordshire County Cricket Club), kept reminding Dad that they needed to leave. Dad was in his element and continued to drink and socialise, surrounded by all the people he knew.

Later that evening, Dad noticed that the Bedford contingent had 'buggered off and left me'. Thankfully, Raymond Way, who played for Wembley and had skippered them previously, managed to drop Dad off at St. Pancras to get the last train home!

Mike Green, who was Chairman and subsequently President of Bedford Town Cricket Club, recalls a Bertie Joel game in the mid-70s. Bedford had been drawn against Southampton CC and, apparently, Mike Rawlinson skippered and Bedford took three car-loads down to the South Coast side, so there was little chance of social distancing! On the return trip, Dad's playing colleagues had decided that they would stop at a pub and try to 'engineer' things so that Dad would have to buy a round of drinks; basically planning that Dad would go in first and they would follow. Dad went to the bar and ordered his light and bitter, but by the time the players had also entered, Dad had already settled up and casually mentioned that the bar snacks were worth a look at! The players' plan to get Dad to buy a full round had backfired, much to Dad's and their amusement. Dad had got away with it again.

Clearly, the good-humoured banter was always there. Friendly, light-hearted joking that fuelled the team spirit.

The annual Car Treasure Hunt was another enjoyable and entertaining experience to look forward to. Packed cars would set off at different intervals to zigzag through the Bedfordshire country lanes; starting and finishing some hours later at the Bury.

Typically, it would be one or more of the teachers who would prepare the route and set out the cryptic clues a few days earlier, ensuring that the route usually involved a few village pub locations.

Looking back with Dad, it must have resembled a scene out of Hanna-Barbera's *Wacky Races*. Rest assured, the Ant Hill Mob-equivalent vehicle (which I thought was called the 'Ampthill Mob', until I was about ten) would usually have Bluey Thomas on board. The occasional clue would somehow miraculously disappear, resulting in some cars being misled. That was almost accepted as being part of the fun. Upon reflection though, we're not too sure about the carbon footprint.

Dad recalls that during a game at the Bury, the home side would put out chairs in front of the pavilion, on the neat lawn to the left of the central path, so as to avoid blocking the view of the game for the mature spectators, who would sit just in front of the kitchen window.

Typically, newspapers and weekend magazines would cover the grass in front of the players' chairs. Conversations would range from serious politics through to the most humorous of stories.

Whoever was next in to bat would remain padded up and it was always very funny when a few wickets tumbled in quick succession and there were occasional cries of 'Who's nicked my bat?' or 'I need to borrow a box, mine's got a crack in it!' as players panicked to get ready to go out and bat. Indeed, during the 1980s, a plastic duck suddenly appeared in the home dressing room and it would occasionally appear in someone's kitbag, which wasn't ideal for mental preparation ahead of going in to bat.

Looking across the ground and just above the pavilion entrance was the large square-cased clock with its black hands set against a white background, presented by Geoff Millman following the original completion of the pavilion building. Just under the canopy was the suspended brass bell, which was used to forewarn the players that the game was about to re-start, typically after the tea interval.

Dad smiles as he remembers that the clock was used constantly during the game, however: the 'last twenty overs' were often crucial in deciding a game's outcome. He reckons that when he was bowling with Dave Eldridge they could easily manage 'twenty-four' overs. Those extra overs were often needed to wrap up the tail!

Frinton

Ron Gale also owned Bentley Lodge, on the sea front at Frinton, which became a regular holiday destination for our family, as well at his Whitehall Court flat on the Thames, which was perfectly situated for the theatre, Royal Festival Hall and the West End. Ron was also close to a number of other families: the Armstrongs, the Watsons, the Stevens and the Perrys. At the time, Chris Perry was Bursar at BMS and Sally was the inspirational swimming coach at BMS. All the families would stay at either location from time to time. Ron clearly enjoyed the company of his 'adopted' families and seeing others enjoying themselves: for us, it was an opportunity to escape and experience a touch of grandeur.

Dad was driving a white Ford Zephyr by the late 1970s, complete with his favourite, memorable number plate: '68

Shy'. He was still driving the car in 1979, when he dropped in to see the Brigadier.

Dad used part of the net sale proceeds from the Queen Alexandra Road sale to buy a new property just off Tyne Crescent, used as an investment property, which he held on to for a couple of years. Dad recalls one of his tenants being Sally Cooley.

In 1979, Dad moved our family into 1 Queens Close, the converted stable and barns opposite the farmhouse in Oakley.

That same year, Pat Briggs asked Dad he if could help with the Bedford School ground, covering for Norman Cooley at the time. The School Bursar knew that Dad was driving for a living and was happy for him to work on the ground during the time he wasn't undertaking Oakley's Carriers work: and so a new chapter would begin...

Bedford School (1980s)

School Shop

In 1980, Dad was offered a full-time role as assistant Bedford School Shop Manager to Derek Smith. The shop stood just outside the impressive black wrought-iron school gates on Burnaby Road, close to the school. Previously, Bob Caple had run a sports shop out of the same building.

Dad sold the Commer Van and bought a black MG Maestro, which would eventually be passed on to my brother Stephen. Car recycling within the Oakley family would become a regular occurrence over the years. A dark-blue Toyota Corolla – Dad recites the PUR 22R plate as if he's recalling a memorable bowling performance – was also passed on to my older brother.

I remind Dad of my first car, a powder-blue Vauxhall Viva HC 1256, that I bought from a BMS school friend around the same time, which became a mechanical work-in-progress project as it broke down on a weekly basis. However, the electrical aerial was the talk of the sixth form, while its most important accessories, in constant use, were the tow-rope and jump leads. Dad would somehow get me home and I always did wonder what the 'HC' stood for: in hindsight, it could have simply been *honestly crap*.

The respected J and A Beagley and Co, a traditional tailor's shop on St Peter's Street, supplied the uniforms for Bedford School. The lease was expiring and Bedford School saw it as an excellent opportunity to take control of their own supplies.

The late Derek Smith, who had worked for Beagley's, was highly experienced, so the school kept him on to manage at the new site and all the remaining shop contents were moved to the Burnaby Road Shop.

Dad recollects that Derek loved his tennis and his weekends would be spent supporting his wife Margaret and their children at the Bradgate Road Tennis Club. The tennis club, with its two red clay courts and ten lawn courts, alongside its purpose-built badminton hall, was converted into housing in the 1990s. Recently, Dad was walking along the embankment and came across a bench looking across the River Ouse that was dedicated to Derek and Margaret.

The school shop was developed further to include stationery items as well as all the school's clothing and sportswear. Many a time I would walk from Bedford Modern School in the early 1980s, more than likely following a net practice session with Andy Curtis and my 1st XI mates, to pop in and see Dad in the shop for a brew. I always noticed that a steady flow of Bedford School pupils would call in to the shop, seeking pen refills, fluorescent markers, protractors and geometry sets: it was like having a mini WH Smith on your doorstep.

The pupils boarding at school had to sign a chit, like an IOU, that would be collated by the House Master, with the parents being billed at the end of each term.

The late Bob Caple stayed on as the resident Cricket Pro, coaching the School 1st XI. He would return to South Africa every winter and come back to Bedford School for the cricket season. He was also coaching the St Alban's College side in Pretoria, so really had the best of both worlds. In fact, he wouldn't permanently return to his beloved South Africa until 1996. The founding headmaster of the Pretorian School, Anton Murray, was a Springbok cricketer and their Head Boy, Gerald Dros, went on to play first-class cricket, skippering South Africa A team and playing for Ireland.

Interestingly, 'Luther Van Dros' (as Bob referred to him), came over to Bedford School in 1992, stayed over with Dad for his first evening and then stayed at the school, playing for their 1st XI. Dad recalls that 'Drossy' was an excellent fielder and never dropped a catch. However, opposing teams were concerned about the school's use of overseas players, similar to the concept of 'ringers'. He even played for the Ousels in the Hospital Cup final in 1992, losing to a Queens Park XI who had raised their game. Dad reckons that Drossy stayed on at the school for an extra couple of months as an electrician's mate!

Pat Briggs would continue to be master-in-charge of sport at the school.

A number of the teachers would call in to the school shop on a regular basis to have a catch-up with Dad. They valued his cricketing knowledge and he was respected. Frequent visitors to the shop included Classics teacher Dave Jarrett, who was the first to gain cricket Blues for both Oxford and Cambridge, and who played for Bedfordshire CCC. Dad's aware that Dave played for Oxford in the Imran Khan era. Dave also played for the Bedford hockey team that shared the Goldington Bury. Dave would become the master-in charge of cricket at Bedford School, so had a lot in common with Dad. He left in 1997 to become headmaster of the famous Reeds School in Surrey.

The late Guy Fletcher was another master-in-charge of sport, after Pat Briggs. Guy had been a student at Bedford School previously, and had played for Bedford Blues at rugby. Dad recalls that he was simply known as 'Fletch' and was loved by everyone. Often, he would be seen helping with the umpiring and just loved all sports.

Tim Machin, master-in-charge of hockey and good batsman, would occasionally nip into the school shop to discuss cricket. His son Gareth would also go to Bedford

School and become a Bedford Town CC player in the late 1980s.

The late Robin Fletcher had arranged tours for the Bedford Town in the 1970s, and played for Bedford Town CC and the Ousels team. He could be seen occasionally enjoying a crafty fag in the car park, as well as leaning forward for a puff on 'that' chair in the showers, while recuperating from a long day in the field.

Dad recites with real excitement a midweek Ousel's XI from the 1980s, which he felt could have represented a Minor Counties team:

Tim Firth – opening bowler
Bob Caple – bowler
Harry Hammond – batsman
Russell Jones w/k and batsman
Pat Briggs – batsman
Norman Cooley – w/k and batsman
Guy Fletcher – batsman
Robin Fletcher – slow left arm
Tim Machin – batsman
Kim Jones (Headmaster) - batsman
Dad - wily off-spinner

Dad had an agreement with shop manager Derek that he could practise in the nets on Tuesday and Thursday afternoons. Whether it was with the U14, U15 or 1st XI, Dad enjoyed getting involved immensely and always kept his boots and cricket jumper in the boot of his car.

It was these regular net sessions that inspired Dad to complete his NCA Basic Coaching badge, which he completed at Redbourne School, Ampthill, under the auspices of Sid Morris.

In the early 1980s, the Bedford School Headmaster asked Dad if he would mind doing some occasional driving for the school. In 1981, the School 1st XI had toured Australia, where they had played against Prince Albert College, Adelaide. A young, very gifted Chris Linke was playing in that game for the home side. That particular school had seen the three Chappell brothers pass through it. Both Ian and Greg became Australian skipper, so Chris came from a school with strong pedigree and history.

Bedford School had agreed to accommodate Chris in 1982 and Dad drove down to pick him up from Heathrow airport. The talented 17-year-old would play for Bedford Town CC and spent considerable time in the school shop speaking to Dad, when he wasn't practising with the 1st XI in the nets.

Dad recalls taking Chris to the Bedford Club in De Parys Avenue. Dad had to lend Chris a jacket and tie, as casual attire was not allowed in the club. They played snooker upstairs and Dad remembers that Chris found the jacket a 'little tight' for his physique!

Chris also played for Bedford Town and would always joke with Dad in his Aussie accent: 'How do you do it, old man?' He was implying that all Dad had to do was to toss the ball up and the batsman would hole out at 'cow corner', yet Chris, as a quick bowler, had to put in all the effort, running in to the wicket off a long run-up! Aah, bless him!

Chris returned to England in 1987 to see some friends in London and made time to meet up again with Dad, which Dad really appreciated, because Chris had put himself out to do it.

In 1982, Dad moved from 46 High Street, Oakley, and into the converted barns opposite: 1 Queens Close. The barn and stables conversion was completed by Les and Tony Sugars (Gambriel and Sugars), the local builders, and paid for by Ron Gale. I made a little money during the summer cleaning bricks for them to re-use.

Ron kept his 1952 Bentley HEW 777 in the old barn conversion, so Dad had to put in place two large railway sleepers, as the gate entrance was slightly elevated, to accommodate it. Ron agreed that Dad should occasionally start it, turn it over and 'give it a run' on the farm track down to the river and back. Anyone driving at those time between Oakley and Pavenham villages, looking up the hill to the south side of the river, would have probably had to look twice on sight of that beautiful beast moving between the wheat fields.

While living at Queens Close, Dad put up Paul Walker, an Australian lad from Perth, who was on an exchange/secondment with Bedford School. He played for Bedford Town CC and Dad remembers one evening when Paul suddenly fainted – nothing to do with Mum's cooking – and keeled over in the hallway, just outside the kitchen. However, subsequently we found out that Dad had given him one of those large Yankee cigars. Thankfully, he didn't hurt himself, recovered fully and was back playing at the weekend.

Dad smiles as he remembers how the young prep school cricketers would be constantly calling in to the school shop to add a new coloured rubber to their bat handle! Dad became quite proficient at using the handle 'stool' and was always keen to help them out.

During the 1980s, various reps would call into the shop to meet up with Dad and try to market their wares.

John Price, the England and Middlesex opening bowler who retired in 1975, would call in representing Slazenger. Dad and John would both play for the 40 Club against the school. Whenever the 40 Club or the MCC would have a fixture at the school and were a player light, they would pop in to see Dad and check his availability!

Also, during the 1960s, Bedford Town CC played against Wembley, on a Sunday fixture, where John played against Dad. Even at club level, John was 'very sharp': however, he always kept it up to the bat at club level and was well respected. Every couple of months John would call in to the shop. John always referred to Dad as 'Sport': 'Hello Sport!' John would always say on arrival.

Brian Lara popped in once, and signed a giant poster. He was giving a talk to the prep school and at the time was building his reputation for 'Lara Bats'. Little did we know then, that in 1994, he would be cleaned up cheaply by twenty-five-year-old Matt White, son of Dick White, a long-term Bedford Town CC member and OBM, bowling for the county in a NatWest game against Warwickshire at Edgbaston. Dad and I were at Edgbaston to witness 'that' ball, which met with a deafening sound of celebration in our spectators' camp and drink was spilt as the realisation gripped us all. Unfortunately, Dick and his wife Maggie were away abroad on holiday, having booked their trip months before!

County Bats would be a regular supplier to Bedford School and Dad would visit them at their High Street, Huntingdon, workshop. He recalls walking up the narrow stairs, being greeted by the distinct smell of raw linseed oil and a vast number of wall-to-wall bats, ranging in weight, size, and handle length. By the end of the 1980s they would be sponsoring my younger brother when he was playing for the County U19 XI.

The charismatic Bill Heath, an ex-Lincoln City Goalkeeper, supplied the school with jackets and trousers. He was also a regular visitor to the shop.

Dad remembers a young, talented Andy Gomarsall coming into the shop when a pupil. He went on to play for Wasps, Bedford Blues and a number of Premier League rugby teams, as well as representing England, and being awarded an MBE. Dad recalls that he was awarded a bat for achieving a knock of 100 during his last innings at school. He went to the school shop to claim his prize, which was to be presented by the headmaster in front of the school during assembly.

During the 1980s, Dad continued to play the occasional representative game for the Gents of Beds XI, which was made up of local club players of standing. Dad recalls Bob Gray from Henlow playing: he also went on to run the Beds County League, played on Sundays. Other players that would represent the side occasionally included Chris Whiting from Bedford Town CC and Pete Bichener, who had played for the county team. He was also a dental mechanic, who fixed Dad's teeth through the years!

Dad fondly recollects the Gents of Beds games against the Bedford Modern School XI. I would be playing against Dad and in our pre-match preparation, Andy Curtis BMS Cricket Coach would tell my fellow team players to look out for Peter Oakley's 'arm ball' – 'It tends to be his fifth delivery most overs.' When I was at the crease playing against Dad, the arm ball was always a decent weapon, but it usually drifted slightly away to the right-hander and often caught out the keeper. It was his '23-yarder' that was bowled almost before you were ready, and that could be lethal! Dad remembers the rare occasion when an umpire would pass comment that they struggled to see him bowl so far back: 'Do that again and I'll no-ball you!'

Dad's typical, orthodox action had a natural lovely loop to it, allowing him to give the ball plenty of air, while enabling him to deliver a venomous clockwise rotating 'cherry'. Many a batsman's eyes would light up and they would get under the ball, not quite getting to the pitch, be fooled by the trajectory, not getting the distance that they had anticipated, and get caught in the field. Also, I remember watching Dad when I was young and a lot of his wickets were stumpings: 'Stumped Hill bowled Oakley' in the 1980s was a regular occurrence, as 'stumped Cooley bowled Oakley' had been in the 1970s!

Record
The year 1982 proved to be a defining one. Ray Stokes, Bedford Town CC Club Secretary, announced at the Club Dinner that Dad had amassed 1,932 wickets since playing

for the Town, with 95 wickets in that current season, and that 'Peter would no doubt pass through 2,000 wickets for the Club by the end of the 1983 season.'

Dad had broken the record for the Northants League with 72 wickets (beating the long-standing 71 tally of wickets record held by G Draper, Kettering Town CC, from 1965, and S. Brown, Rushton Town CC, from 1978. Little did anyone know that Dad would continue to play for another ten years (and I would get him to turn out for me, on the odd occasion when someone had dropped out at short notice, for the Sunday 1st XI in the late 1990s). He's certain that he would have finally returned in the region of 3,000 wickets before hanging up his 'playing boots' for the Town.

That same year Dad picked up his third 'nine-fer'. Dad's figures against Irthlingborough IIs are simply amazing: 23 overs, 9-27. Dad, with a beaming smile on his face, felt he was unplayable on their track. Irthlingborough were bowled out for just 67. David Eldridge OB, who bowled a flatter, much pacier off-spin, picked up the other wicket, 1-21. David was another regular Bedford Town player, who had a distinctive, infectious laugh, and his sons, David junior, Chris and Simon would all go on to play for the club.

In that game 'Powelly' skippered, and other players included Lugsdin, Davidson, Price, O'Dwyer, Newman, Fensome, Hardman, and David Pratt – all regular Bedford Town CC contributors during the 1970s and 1980s.

Some of Dad's magical figures in 1982, as Dad recites them with immense joy, from old newspaper cuttings include: 14 overs, 10 maidens, 5-4 against Great Oakley in the Northants County League.

Against Berkhamsted, a Sunday 1st XI fixture, Dad ended up bowling ten overs, four maidens, 3-9. He reads through the team playing on that day: Ian Peck (another OB) scored a 'cracking' ton; Dave Jarrett, playing for the

Town, rattled up a tasty 54; and Malcolm Wynn and Bluey Thomas were also playing that afternoon.

Dad recalls that in May 1982, a huge amount of preparation had gone into getting the Bedford School ground ready for an important first-class county game: Northants were playing Lancashire in the John Player Competition. The inspirational Clive Lloyd was leading the Lancashire side and was at the school ground, along with Geoff Cook, his opposing skipper for Northants, who would go onto play seven Test matches for England, and serve as coach at Durham. He also still holds the Northants County record score of 344, clocked up in a second-wicket partnership with Robin Boyd-Moss OB. Dad recalls that Robin was a great friend of Ian Peck: both products of a very strong 1970s Bedford School set-up.

Unfortunately, the heavens opened: serious, terrible weather, including hailstones, which resulted in that game having to be postponed, leaving players and spectators frustrated. This happened a few times throughout Dad's playing career.

Current Bedfordshire County CC President Russell Beard OBM, reminds Dad of a Northants County League game in the early 1980s. Russell was driving Dad in his own yellow Mini to an early season game. The weather was atrocious and they got stuck behind a gritting lorry, much to their amusement and frustration. Apparently, conditions didn't improve, the be-spectacled Mike Rawlinson, who was opening the batting, had to come off due to snow getting in the way of his vision!

Dad talks very highly about Norman Cooley, head groundsman at Bedford School, and smiles when he remembers Norman pointing out one of his groundsman colleagues, who had fallen asleep on the tractor, on the far side of the school ground. He'd driven through the hedge into Pemberley Avenue, before realising what he had just done. Thankfully, no one was injured.

Dad also fondly remembers Chris Proudman OBM: left-arm opening bowler and a great character, who usually had a word or two to say about the game, occasionally while puffing away on his pipe after a good game for the Town. Chris also played for Bedfordshire CCC in the mid-1980s.

Towards the late 1980s (and into the 1990s), Dad remembers that left-hand opening bat Phil Thomas skippered the Saturday 1st XI, usually arriving for games in flip-flops! Phil had a great personality and a strong northern accent. And then there was the suave Jeff Wood, a useful all-rounder, who would become chairman of the committee.

By 1984, Dad had moved again: into Castle Road, close to the Rothsay Road roundabout, near to Russell Park, where Dad used to muck around with his mates all those years earlier. It was a temporary move, while the Duckmill Crescent apartment was being completed by locally-based SDC Builders.

At that time, the dark-green Vauxhall Astra was traded in for his royal-blue Ford Orion, which he held on to for three years. He enjoyed that car, which had plenty of boot room for his kit, but we remember how my younger brother (who was barely fifteen at the time) sneaked out in the Orion for a brief drive 'around Bedford' without anyone knowing, or so he thought. Having said that, I remind Dad of his early 'less-than-legal' taxi pick-ups for his Dad, all those years earlier.

Dad moved into the elegant 24 Duckmill Crescent apartment in Duckmill Lane, Bedford, in December 1985. It looked over the Great Ouse and embankment to the south side.

In 1987, Derek Smith retired and Dad took on Pam Cromie and Beryl Newman to help out in the school shop, while Dad became the school shop manager, a position that he held for twelve years. The shop went from strength to strength and Dad enjoyed managing his small team, dealing with the school's needs, building professional relationships and finding time to help support and coach the junior teams. He loved all aspects of the job and it brought out all his best qualities. Dad was highly respected, built an excellent reputation and developed a strong, trusted relationship with the school.

Sadly, in 1989, Bedford Grandad passed away and no doubt looks down on Dad, with huge pride, from that TT race in the sky. It was Bedford Grandad who taught Dad to drive, 'constructed' his first car, transported Dad down to Lord's, found him his first residence in Edgware Road, managed to sort out his first job, paid for his wedding reception, provided the mortgage deposit towards his first home and even forgave Dad for the 'burning car' incident! Perhaps Bedford Grandad didn't truly understand the rules of cricket, but he provided the solid platform needed for Dad to succeed in life and for that, Dad remains eternally grateful.

Dad in July 1949 - the year he left School & a year before
entering Lord's Ground Staff

John & Elsie Oakley in 1933 - year before dad's born

Bedford Granadiers 1947

Bedford Granadiers winning Cricket League U14 XI title
1948

Brigadier 1950

Lord s Grounds Staff 1951

Western Command Army XI 1953

Standard 8 – dad's first car he bought 1958

Sharnbrook FC - Beds Intermediate Cup 1959

(Bedford Town CC 1st XI 1963

Australia v Minor Counties, Goldington Bury 1964

Bedford Town Club Game 1965

Town spoil St. Albans' unbeaten record

OAKLEY TAKES 6 FOR 17

WHAT a fascinating game is cricket! That was borne out to the full in the Bedford Town v. St. Albans City match at Goldington Bury on Saturday. No one would have predicted that either side would be dismissed for less than 150.

When the game started, with Bedford taking first knock, predictions were that the skipper would declare at tea time with 200 runs at least for the loss of few wickets. For the outcome the vagaries of the wicket can be blamed to some extent, but so can the glorious uncertainty of cricket.

After Howard had been caught at five from a bad shot to a bad ball, Morris and Chamberlain advanced the score quickly to 38, when Morris was bowled by one that kept rather low.

Hoare's glorious six

Chamberlain continued to bat steadily, but with Hoare unable to pierce a well placed off-side field. Holt bowled four maidens and one over with only one run being scored. Chamberlain was "yorked," but Hoare hit one glorious six into the front of The Bury House. Unhappily, he was bowled in attempting a big hit off a slower ball.

Heaton and Street were both out to most undistinguished shots, as also in a lesser degree were Oakley and Smart. It was left to the last pair, White, who displayed a more than useful batting knowledge, and Breeze, to add 20 most useful runs.

St. Albans started their innings with Hacket and Casey. Breeze bowled a maiden and Oakley, who opened from the opposite end with his off-spinners, rather than the usual two last men—obviously because of the wicket—got Hacket with his second ball. He mis-hit and was well caught by Hoare.

Parren did not last, being well bowled, through the gate, by Oakley. Cooper, a former Hertfordshire County player, stuck in well, as did Hilton. These two took the total from 10 to 71, at which total Cooper was out. He half hit a swinging full toss from White and was well caught at short leg by Heaton.

Two runs later, Hilton was well bowled by Oakley, who had returned to the attack; in fact, in his second spell, Oakley bowled six overs, five of which were maidens, and took four wickets for two runs. There was stout-hearted resistance from Lord and a certain amount from Alcock, but the result was then inevitable. Oakley completed a fine performance by taking six wickets for 17 runs.

The game was distinguished by St. Albans' fine fielding but both Chamberlain and Hoare were dropped. However, as this was the first time St. Albans have been defeated this season, Bedford must be congratulated on a fine performance.

Bedford: E. C. Howard c Baldwin b Cooper 5, W. Chamberlain b L. Holt 25, S. T. Morris b L. Holt 22, D. F. Hoare b L. Holt 34, J. D. Heaton c Baldwin b L. Holt 8, R. W. Street c Lingham b Alcock 0, G. L. B. August lbw b Alcock 8, P. Oakley b L. Holt 3, G. I. Smart c Lingham b Alcock 0, R. White c I. Holt b Cooper 14, F. K. Breeze not out 5, extras 8, total 133.

Bowling: L. Holt 25o. 11m. 41r. 5w.; Cooper 5-0-19-2; Alcock 20-1-65-3.

St. Albans: K. D. Hacker c Hoare b Oakley 0, H. K. Casey c Oakley b Breeze 10, D. G. Parren b Oakley 0, D. V. Cooper c Heaton b White 30, A. Hilton b Oakley 26, P. Lord not out 6, P. Baldwin b Oakley 0, L. J. Holt b Oakley 11, I. Holt b Oakley 0, P. Lingham c Smart b Breeze 0, C. R. Alcock c Hoare b Breeze 6, extras 4, total 95.

Bowling: Breeze 9-4-2-30-3; Oakley 13-6-17-6; White 7-0-24-1; Street 3-0-16-0.

Dad s 6-17 versus St Albans 1965

Stephen Oakley & Phil Hoare – 'on the gangs' 1969

TEAM . . . Bedford's winning line-up. Front (left to right), J. Dalzell, R. White, P. G. Considine, capt., P. D. Oakley, and N. S. Cooley. Back (left to right): C. Head, umpire, P. Swift, M. J. Rawlinson, T. Thomas, R. J. Plowman, B. Stuart, W. J. Bushby, and P. Findley, scorer.

1971 June

● Defeated: Ousels prepare to meet Westfield YC.   Picture: CW77

July 1992

Bedford Town CC 1st XI 1971 & Ousels XI 1992

Bedford Town CC win at Lords - 1975

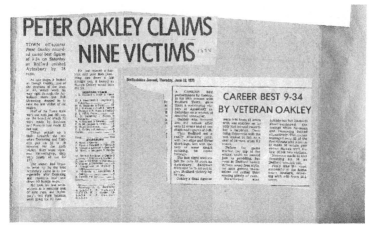

Dad s 9-fer in 1975

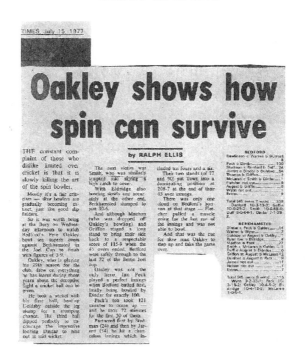

Dad s match-winning figures in 1977

Oakley blitz

1982

But Town still on the rocks

BEDFORD TOWN'S bid to move away from the relegation zone of the Northamptonshire County League suffered another setback on Saturday when their game against Old Wellingburians was a victim of the weather.

But the second eleven improved their chances of winning promotion from the third division by thrashing Great Oakley by 136 runs. There was only one Great Oakley on view at the Bury and that was the Town's wily off spinner Peter Oakley. The visiting batsmen had absolutely no idea of how to play him and he returned the amazing figures of 5-4 in 14 overs, of which 10 were maidens.

David Eldridge and Geoff Irvine gave him good support and Great Oakley, who had been set to score 190, were skittled for just 53.

The only batsman to offer any resistance was opener Dennis Skinner who batted throughout to be unbeaten with 28.

In contrast, the Town batsmen had been in great form with Mike Rawlinson and Stan Purdy, dropped from the first team, seizing the initiative from the start. Rawlinson cracked 64 and Purdy 37, and when they were dismissed, Roger Lugsdin and David Pratt carried on the good work and the Town romped to 189-5 before declaring.

The seconds are in such great form at the moment that it seems that only hangovers from the disco at the clubhouse on Friday evening, which it is hoped every member will attend, will stop them from going to the top by beating Irthlingborough on Saturday.

The first eleven had to settle for a draw with Radlett at the Bury on Sunday.

It was an entertaining match with Radlett recovering from a shaky start to total 180-8 declared. Roger Loft again bowled well to take 5-48.

The Town lost Alan Fordham in the first over when they replied and runs came slowly before tea. But Trevor Thomas stepped up the rate and while he was at the wicket, Bedford were in with a chance.

But when he had cracked 62 he was bowled and it was left to Geoff Irvine and Robin Fletcher to play out time. The Town finished on 156-8...

TICKETS for the Beds-Somerset game at the Bury on July 3 are available.

They can be obtained from either Colin Head of 45, Falcon Avenue, Bedford, or Ray Stokes, of 16 Bridge End, Bromham. Prices are £2 for adults and £1 for students and pensioners and applicants should enclose the correct money and a stamped addressed envelope.

BEDFORD II

M. Rawlinson c Thomas b Bell	64
S. Purdy c Parsons b Bull	37
R. Lugsdin st Parsons b Thomas	46
D. Baldwin c Parsons b Smith	0
D. Pratt not out	28
P. Howe b Smith	2
J. Powell not out	4
Extras	10
Total (for 5 wkts)	**189**

Bowling: A. Smith 16-7-48-2; A. Mann 7 0-51-0; D. Thomas 7 0 41-1; M. York 7-0-26-0; C. Bell 8-0 33 2.

GREAT OAKLEY

C. York c/b Oakley	0
D. Skinner not out	28
C. Bull b Oakley	0
A. Smith c/b Eldridge	0
D. Thomas c Eldridge b Irvine	5
M. York c Lugsdin b Eldridge	4
S. Parsons c Baldwin b Irvine	1
A. Mann b Oakley	0
C. Parsons lbw Oakley	2
D. Giannion lbw Eldridge	0
T. Mann b Oakley	0
Extras	13
Total	**53**

Bowling: P. Howe 7-1-24-0; F. Oakley 14-10-6-5; D. Eldridge 10-3-14-3; G. Irvine 4-0-10-2; D. Pratt 1-1-0-0.

Dad destroys Great Oakley 1982

89

It's an all family affair

● **Proud dad: Pete Oakley with sons John, left, and Andrew at the Bury on Saturday**

IT'S a family affair in Bedford Town seconds these days. Pete Oakley is captain and his sons Andrew and John are his lieutenants, writes Sam Cartmell.

SEP.
1990

On Saturday this amazing cricketing family stole the show.

Andrew got 40 and John 37 not out in the side's 218. Then dad, bowling his deceiving spin, took an astounding six wickets for ten runs. "Oakers" also steered his side to a win over Brondesbury the next day.

Pete, 56, first played for Bedford in 1947 after being on the Lords staff for five years. He played minor county cricket between 1955 and 1974 and is now a respected groudsman, retailer and walking cricket museum at Bedford School.

He speaks fondly of years past: of a golden age in the late 60s and early 70s when giants like Norman Cooley, Dick White and Richard Banks were in their prime.

Links with schools, especially Bedford Modern have produced many stars. Pete recalls Geoff Millman who captained Notts and played for England. Northants run-machine Alan Fordham and former schoolmate Neil Stanley have had some degree of the Oakley treatment.

A new generation of familiar names is the latest to benefit from his wisdom. Matt White and Ben Banks, town and county stars, have continued where their fathers left off. "It's great to see the youngsters come through, especially the sons" says Pete.

All three Oakleys will be in action this weekend as cricketers fight against the dying of the light and the end of the season.

It's a family affair in 1990

90

Dad with Bob Caple & Tony Catt 1991 & with Alastair
Cook 2014

Dad with Derek Randall & Sir Donald Bradman 2004 &
at Bedford School 2003

Dad on the Australian Tour 2004 'coaching & ice cream'

Coaching (1990s)

Although Dad was still playing in the early 1990s, he was also coaching more, trying to give something back to the game he loved.

While Dave Jarrett was looking after the School 1st XI, Dad would continue to help coach the U14 XI and saw some very talented players progress through the ranks.

The team including the exceptionally talented Will Smith, whose Dad owned the Bedford Book Shop opposite Market Square. He went on to play for Nottinghamshire, Durham and Hampshire. Dad remembers Will playing for the County U19 XI as a right-hand bat and off-spinner. Will became Durham captain and scored 925 runs for them in their maiden Championship title in 2008 (retiring in 2019).

Dad fondly remembers too Greg Cruse, a young South African cricketer who came over to join the Bedford School XI in 1991. The previous year Dad and Mum had gone to visit Bob and Jenny Caple in South Africa, enjoying a trip up Table Mountain and staying at a safari lodge on the return trip, at the edge of the Kruger National Park, with Greg's parents.

Dad tells me that they saw out 1991 in Sun City, with all its Las Vegas-style razzle-dazzle.

Every year the Bedfordshire U19 XI would play in the Cambridge Festival, eventually winning the competition in 1999, when Dave Mercer was in charge. Dad enjoyed supporting Bob Gray and the U19 coaching team: an abundance of talented teenagers showing potential for their school and club sides, with the world stage waiting for them, would make their presence known in the U19 squad.

The Bedfordshire County U19 XI squad would always be based at Newnham College Cambridge for the full duration of the festival, and every day they would play a game at a different college ground. Dad remembers that Tim Chapman OB was an excellent skipper of the county team in the 1990s.

Dad remembers that the U19 XI was a great springboard for young, talented players. However, just occasionally, the obvious raw talent would result in the individual perhaps being selected for the full county side, as was the case with Neil Stanley OBM in the late 1980s, who went on to enjoy five seasons at Northants. Dad recalls that Neil's father, Jack Stanley, would assist occasionally with the umpiring.

Another talent identified early on was Alan Fordham. He was a formidable batsman who 'went through with his shots at school', demonstrating a brilliant self-confidence that would typically lead to some big knocks. He left Bedford Modern School to study at Durham University, was quickly snapped up by Northants and is currently working for the ECB.

Paul Owen was another talented OBM, a useful, slow left-armer, who would go into the Beds County XI in the late 1980s before joining Gloucestershire in 1990. Eventually he would return to play for Bedfordshire until 1996. I recall scampering three 'leg byes' off the last ball (deliberately fired into my legs) delivered by Paul against a strong Luton side skippered by Phil Hoare in the late 1990s, to tie the game. Sadly, Paul passed away in June last year, just a day after his 51st birthday.

Toby Bailey was a brilliant wicket keeper who could also bat. Toby played for Bedford School in the early 1990s and Bedford Town CC before playing for Northants in 1996. Toby took over the keeper's gloves from David Ripley, the current Northants coach. Dad reminisces about

Toby, who was a great personality with a good sense of humour and a very fast pair of hands. If the batsman's back foot happened to be over the crease line, even for a fraction of a second, Toby would pounce: he had the ability to create a wicket. He was a sensation at Bedford Town CC and would go on to coach the Argentinian cricket team and then work in Scotland.

Another couple of Bedford Modern School lads played a big part in the Bedfordshire County U19 XI in the early 1990, Dad recalls. Mark Brownridge was a consistent, useful all-rounder while big-hitting Richard Whitbread occasionally dominated bowling attacks. Mark's father also helped with some umpiring from time to time.

Bedford School player Adrian Shankar also showed potential playing for the County U19 XI and then for Lancashire 2nd XI and Worcestershire. Dad recalls an U19 XI game when he spoke to Adrian's Dad and mentioned that he had serious toothache. Dr Shankar managed to get Dad a hospital appointment the following morning at 8.45am. Without a doubt, this was another case of 'who you know'.

I skippered the Sunday 1st XI in the late 1990s, and occasionally Dad would play. We had a rule that if a player dropped out at short notice, rather than pinch a player from the second XI, the player who couldn't play would have to find an alternative. However, this approach didn't prove too successful. Usually, what happened was that I would receive a call late on a Friday evening: 'Apologies, skip, but I can't play on Sunday because my pet hamster needs a trim . . .' My back-up then would be to call Dad. If we were in the field, Dad would simply walk to first slip; if we were short on bowling, Dad could never resist turning his arm over. However, he would usually be unable to release his first ball, and a shout of 'b----- me' would ensue, to the amusement of his fellow players.

In 1992, Dad would lose another Ousels final to an excellent Bedford Asians side, held at the Bedford Modern School. The groundsman was Bobby Folds, who had played for the Bedford Eagles Football, as well as Gillingham, and Northampton Town and Dad recalls Bobby being a useful left-hand bat.

Dad recites some of his fellow players on the day including:

- Drossy
- Cooley
- Machin
- Younger brother Jon
- Russell Jones
- Harry Hammond

The late 1990s saw Ollie Clayson OBM play for the Bedfordshire U19 XI. Ollie was a talented bat who could also bowl off-breaks, exhibiting a similar technique to Dad's. In 1999, he got his debut for Bedfordshire CCC and never looked back, being a regularly selected member of the county side throughout the 2000s.

Another useful young player who played for the Bedfordshire U19 XI and went on to play regularly for Bedfordshire CCC for several years was Will Sneath. Dad recalls Will was a very talented all-rounder who went on to play for Northants 2nd XI. Will is now a committee member for Bedfordshire CCC.

Monty Panesar was one of the most famous OBMs, who started playing for Bedfordshire U19 XI in the late 1990s. Monty played in the Cambridge Festival final at the tender age of 18, when Bedfordshire U19 XI won the competition. The team would then play the winners of the Oxford equivalent competition, and lost to Herefordshire. However, Monty was a gifted slow left arm finger spinner, who would go on to bigger and better things! Monty played for the England U19 XI and then for Northants,

97

Sussex, and Essex during his first-class county career. In 2006, Monty made his test debut for England and never looked back. Although Dad points out, however, that despite Monty's success at national level, he didn't quite manage a nine-fer across three decades (sorry, Monty!).

Dad fondly mentions Sean Davey, who was a teacher and house master at Bedford School in the late 1980s into the 1990s. Dad recollects that Sean was a good all-round sportsman, playing for Bedford Town CC and the Ousels. He had a bubbly, confident personality and a distinctive northern accent, and ended up refereeing English rugby at the game's highest level.

Bob Caple retired in 1996 and returned home to South Africa. Bob would complete another couple of seasons coaching in South Africa before hanging up his bowling boots.

In 1999, Dad formally retired from managing the school shop. However, he continued on a part-time basis, helping to coach a variety of school sides on Tuesday and Thursday afternoons. He also joined the teams on their match days, travelling with them, encouraging the young players to show their talent, be brave and 'give it a go'. This extension and continued involvement with the game he loved, helping to pass on his experience, kept Dad young at heart.

Bedford Rowing Club

Dad enjoyed his retirement party and also special birthdays at Bedford Rowing Club, situated above Bedford Boat Club. Dad and Lynn would frequent the rowing club for its events and social functions on a regular basis. Usually on Friday and Saturday evenings during the summer, they could go out on to the long balcony, which looked over the Great River Ouse, and admire the spectacular view: the historic Town Bridge illuminated and its reflection shimmering on the river. Dad recalls some great evenings at the club, leading to occasionally dancing the night away and then staggering 'all 100 yards' back to Duckmill Crescent!

Another regular visitor to the rowing club was Martin Watson, who also had a van business like Dad's. Martin had sold Dad that Standard 8, Dad's first car that he'd bought when he worked at Nicholls on the old Kingsway site. He lived close by on Cardington Road and Dad recalls that he liked to smoke. When the indoor smoking ban was introduced, he would nip out to the balcony: so the balcony had other uses, apart from offering fantastic views across the river.

Over the years, the balcony would become a popular a filming point for several television programmes. It provided the perfect view: the Town Bridge, and the majestic Swan Hotel built by the Duke of Bedford in the 18th Century in the background, on the north side of the Great Ouse. Interestingly, the local BBC Look East News still starts its daily programme with a scene involving rowers on the Ouse, the Town Bridge in the distance, with the numerous weeping willow trees overhanging the banks and forming a natural defence against river erosion.

When a rowing event took place, Dad would help with directing the traffic to a temporary car park close to Longholme Lake (also known as the boating lake), further along the Embankment. Dad recalls parking was quite tight and spaces were at a premium. Without a little help and guidance, people would occasionally struggle to find a space, so Dad was always keen to assist where he could.

Every Friday night, a decent crowd would gather for the well-regarded meat raffle which, Dad fondly remembers, was only £1 a ticket. Interestingly, Dad would be a frequent winner and clearly worked out that the odds for winning were pretty good!

A great friend of Dad's was Jason Crowe, who lived in Duckmill Lane very close to the rowing club. Jason had been a lifeguard at the local swimming pool and also a fireman. Dad remembers that Jason was on duty at Bedford School that early Sunday morning in 1979, when the main hall was subject to an arson attack. More recently, the gloriously restored Bedford School Great Hall was home to Captain Sir Tom Moore's 100th birthday cards.

Sir Tom's RAF flypast, including a Mark IX Spitfire, also passed over Bedford. Speaking to Dad that weekend, he thought we (his three sons) had arranged the flypast for his own 86th birthday, as it was the same day, 30th April! We were very sad to hear about Captain Sir Tom's death as this story is being finalised. His funeral took place at Bedford Crematorium, only a mile or so away from the Goldington Bury. He made a huge difference to the world, inspired many and enjoyed an interest in cricket along the way.

Jason had his own engineering, heating and boiler business, and would help Dad out over the years at the Duckmill apartment. Jason had a penthouse apartment in the idyllic village of Alcossebre in Spain, and Dad would eventually buy his own Spanish second home, in the same coastal retreat, in 2006.

John Mingay was very much the key person who managed the rowing club. John was a councillor for Newnham for a number of years and Dad mentions that he was awarded Bedford Alderman status in 2020 for his dedication and services to the Town.

Dad recalls too Jack Pope, a retired bomber pilot, who managed the Bedford Blues Rugby Supporters Club. Jack would typically be in the rowing club most evenings and a plaque was put up on the wall next to where he used to sit, following his death in 2003.

Tom and Hilda Gardener would also become friends of Dad's and Lynn's. Hilda, coincidentally, had worked for Sydney Press in the 1960s and Tom would become a school groundsman for the county council, including working on the square at the Goldington Bury in the early 1980s. They were also keen members of the Bedford Conservative Club on Cardington Road. Tom is currently 94 and Dad and Lynn help out with his care, popping around to see him on a weekly basis. Tom was groundsman at Goldington Secondary School when my brother Stephen was there, and the fields would back onto Bedford Grandad's garden in Brookfield Road.

Dad would officially retire in 1999 and collect his State pension: however, would continue helping the Bedford School cricket coaching staff on a part-time basis for a further sixteen wonderful years.

Millennium to date

Dad was presented with some leaving gifts in the Bedford School Staff Common Room in April 1999: little did they know that he would continue to support the school through to 2016! Master in charge of cricket at the time was Jeremy Farrell.

Bedford School maintained good links with Nottinghamshire CCC. Richard Bates, who was a useful off-spinner, joined them at the end of his cricketing career with Notts in the late 1990s. Dad speaks very highly about Richard's contribution in 1998. He would go on to coach the England Women's Team in 2003.

Andy Pick, previously an opening bowler for Nottinghamshire, was 1st XI Bedford School Cricket Coach and also had a positive impact on the standard of cricket in 1999. After leaving Bedford School, Andy would become the England U19 XI coach from 2004 and then went on to work for the Canadian Cricket Association in 2006.

Derek Randall

The wonderfully talented England cricketer Derek Randall arrived on the scene in 2001. He had played for Nottinghamshire and England, retiring from first-class county cricket in 1993 then played for Suffolk and coached the Cambridge University Cricket XI.

Dad recalls an early encounter with Derek in the dining halls. John Springall, yet another ex-Lord's Ground staff colleague of Dad's, who went on to play for Nottinghamshire CCC, was a down-to-earth Londoner with a matching cockney accent. He was also a really useful right-hand bat, who could bowl as well, and he ended up playing 119 matches for Nottinghamshire CCC.

Unbelievably, Derek said that he had played in John's final game for Notts as a teenager, in the late 1960s, and recalls Dad's old ground staff colleague: that definitely 'broke the ice' with Derek.

Interestingly, John stayed good friends with Geoff Millman OBM, another ex-Notts cricketer, and became a very successful market trader after packing up cricket. Dad remembers John driving him to the 50th reunion of the Lord's Ground staff in 2000. Geoff lent John his own car, knowing that John didn't drink alcohol. Sadly, the chirpy cockney passed away early last year.

Derek and Dad became good friends over the years and would go on the Bedford School cricket tour to Australia, and to Grenada in the Caribbean with the Old England XI, who were playing against the Old West Indies side. Derek would stay on at Bedford School for a further ten years, and he and Dad still keep in touch.

In 2006, Alan Lamb skippered the Old England team against the Old West Indies XI. Dad remembers Alan always joking with his fellow team members and keeping their spirits up. Alan had been the guest speaker at Bedford Town's club dinner on a couple of occasions and always had a humorous story to tell, in his distinct South African accent, with the occasional added expletive!

Others players in the Old England squad who had represented their country down the years included: Rob Bailey, ex-Northants; Peter Such, off-spinner with Essex; left arm over John Lever; middle-order bat John Morris ex-Derbyshire; opening bowler ex-Worcestershire Neal Radford; and Chris Lewis, the talented all-rounder, just a couple of years before his regrettable Gatwick Airport episode.

Derek would go on to invite Dad to a one-day Old England XI versus Old Australia XI at Trent Bridge. Derek organised a private box for Dad: apparently, the bar staff constantly topped up his glass as he watched Derek hit a tasty half-century. I can imagine Dad would have been in his element!

Derek lived on site in one of the Bedford School houses. Dad socialised with Derek, brought him over to Oakley Cricket Club and Biddenham Cricket Club, and introducing Derek to some of his social and cricketing connections.

Dad and Derek occasionally enjoyed a round of golf at the Biddenham Golf Club. Over the years, Derek would also invite Dad to numerous matches at Trent Bridge to watch Nottinghamshire play, especially the Twenty-20 games. They clearly enjoyed each other's company.

In 2005, Dad recalls taking Derek over to Olney CC to formally open their new pavilion. They turned up wearing their Australian tour blazers and a good evening was had by all.

So, as the story goes, Bedford School were light on supervisors for the cricket nets for various age levels within the Upper School. The school contacted Dad to see whether he could help out and as you would imagine, Dad jumped at the chance!

Alastair Cook

In the late 1990s, a talented young boy by the name of Alastair Cook was passing through the ranks. Alastair had joined Bedford School at the age of 13 on a music scholarship.

Dad recalls that Alastair was only fourteen when he notched up an impressive 100 for an MCC XI, who had been one man short during their annual game against the School 1st XI. Apparently, the MCC needed an extra player and had spoken to Jeremy Farrell ahead of the game, to see who could help out.

Dad smiles when he recalls that Derek would have Alastair facing the bowling machine, while Dad would be 'turning his arm over' in the nets, despite being now in his late 60s. There's a wonderful quote from Derek in *The Guardian* in 2010: 'I helped Alastair as a young boy, but he gave me more pleasure at this school than I gave him help, if I'm honest . . .'

Alastair left Bedford School in 2003 to join Essex CCC. He had been on Keith Fletcher's radar for some time and turned professional with them, under the auspices of the great Graham Gooch. Dad recalls that Alastair broke lots of Bedford School cricketing records, taking the bar to a higher level. He was also the England U19 XI captain before going on to do brilliant things for England as a player and skipper. Dad's adamant that Alastair's achievements, more importantly, served as a wonderful inspiration to all the youngsters he helped to coach. Alastair had reached the highest pinnacle, so why couldn't they?

Dad shows me a couple of signed copies of books that Alastair has subsequently written, including his recent autobiography, which Alastair had given to Dad. Dad is very proud of Alastair's handwritten comments and references about his coaching support while at Bedford School. With a cheeky smile, he's looking forward to providing Alastair with a signed copy of this book!

Dad raises a smile when he recalls Sky TV arriving at Bedford School on the back of Alastair's budding Test cricket success. He was called into the pavilion for an interview to provide a few comments regarding Alastair's dedication to the game while at School. A friend called Ian King, who lived opposite Dad in Alcossebre, Dad's Spanish retreat, subsequently saw the interview clip on television and was impressed with his comments and fame: it was the talk of the Spanish village!

<u>Staying with Jon and fast cars</u>

Dad began to spend more time with my younger brother Jonathan (Jon) and his family in Essex.

Jon had been a talented cricketer but his true passion, encouraged by Dad, was driving fast cars. Jon had been a go-karting champion in his younger days and was 'fearless' when in the driving seat.

Dad proudly recalls Jon gaining his racing licence at Jonathan Palmer's Racing School, at the Bedford Autodrome, Thurleigh. However, it's Jon's actual driving that Dad 'relives': Jon once took Dad around Silverstone for a couple of laps in a rather quick Porsche. I sense it had been like sitting beside the late Donald Campbell CBE, during a record-breaking speed attempt!

Another time, Jon asked Dad to follow him to Spa (the famous Spa-Francorchamps Circuit to be precise) in Belgium. Jon provided a Porsche for Dad and then Jon drove an updated model, leading the way. They managed to arrive in Belgium in very good time: I reckon the journey probably resembled a scene from *The Italian Job*!

The following day, Jon was testing his new model on the track, taking the car to its limits when, unfortunately, the engine blew!

While at the Spa circuit, Dad was taken for a ride around the track in an open-top Caterham 7. Dad recalls the feeling of being pinned back into his seat and being completely open to the elements, apart from the tiny windscreen!

Thankfully, they managed to return home safely a few days later in Dad's vehicle. Jon's passion for fast cars hasn't diminished and the family's interest in cars has clearly been passed down the generations.

Australian Tour

Jeremy Farrell invited Dad to join the Australian Tour party in 2004. Dad thoroughly enjoyed the three-week trip, centred around Sydney and Melbourne. Dad recalls travelling up to Bowral in the southern highlands area of New South Wales, where Sir Donald Bradman lived and played his club cricket in the 1920s. The Bradman Oval is now a heritage-listed ground and Dad and Derek had their photograph taken either side of the Bradman statue.

So, the story goes, when Dad and Derek arrived at Bowral, they were playing Derek's scintillating 174 knock from 1977 for England against the Aussies in the Centenary Test at the MCG, on their screen. What a welcome!

Derek was then invited to attend a breakfast session at the MCG on Boxing Day and watch the Aussies play Pakistan. Dad tells me the breakfast took place in the famous 'Legends Room'. Dean Jones attended, along with a number of other top Australian cricketers mixed in with a few Australian politicians and dignitaries.

Dad was given a security lanyard and a small clock as a memento, engraved with the date of the event. The lanyard remains on Dad's bedroom door handle to this day and every morning he is able to remind himself of that wonderful occasion., The clock sits even nearer to Dad, on his bedside cabinet, together with the photograph of Dad and Derek sitting alongside the Bradman Statue.

Dad was also given a couple of Matthew Hayden-endorsed Gray Nicholls cricket balls signed personally by Dean Jones and Dad subsequently gave one to me. Dean sadly passed away in September last year, having suffered a massive heart attack, aged only 59. Dean was a brilliant Australian batsman, who could also bowl the occasional off-spinner and who is sadly missed by all.

When Dad was in Australia, he contacted Alf Tasker, who, with his brother Alan, had been with Dad on the Lord's Ground staff back in the 1950s.

They had emigrated in the 1960s as 'Ten Pound Poms': the Assisted Passage Migration Scheme. Interestingly, both famous English fast bowlers, Harold Larwood (1950) and Frank Tyson (1960), took advantage of the scheme when they retired from cricket.

Dad managed to make contact with Alf Tasker, who excitedly turned up to a game. He could see Dad walking around the boundary with Derek, and spoke to Dad for ages, reminiscing about some great times they had enjoyed at Lord's. Later, Alf picked up Dad from his hotel to meet his wife Margaret. Dad tells me that Alf and his future wife had met on the boat trip across, and that they lived locally in Bentleigh, a suburb of Melbourne. Alf had also managed to attend the 50th Lord's Ground staff reunion in 2000. Dad has recently received a delayed Christmas card from Margaret, advising him that sadly, Alf died in 2019, and had always talked fondly about Dad.

Following the Tour, Dad found himself in a slightly embarrassing situation having taken his camera into the Photographic Shop on Tavistock Street, Bedford. Mike Lord, the proprietor, who was a good friend of my brother's, opened up the back and found out that no film had been loaded into the camera! Thankfully, another Bedford School teacher who had joined the Tour party with his young family, was able to provide copies of his own photos, kindly mounted into an album for Dad.

Dad recalls a talented teenager on that Australian Tour, Alex Wakely. A strong right-hand batsman, Alex had left Bedford School in 2007. He captained the England U19 XI and currently plays for Northants and has skippered them for a few years. Dad's aware that Alex's testimonial year has had to be unfortunately postponed to 2021, due to the impact of the Covid pandemic.

Alex bought Dad's lovely white Vauxhall Signum car in the year he left Bedford School. The car had Dad's personalised plate of A9 PJO and Dad decided that he would leave the plates on the car for Alex.

Interestingly, Dad's current vehicle, a Peugeot 308 GT Line, has the number plate OA11 LEY, which Dad believes is even closer to the family name.

Dad owned a dark-blue Honda Accord in 2000 and traded that in for a blue Mazda 6, which he then held for a couple of years. The Mazda was eventually traded in for the smart Signum that would eventually catch Alex's eye.

Dad smiles when he remembers when Headmaster Kim Jones asked if he could use the School vehicle to pick up the indefatigable Ann Widdecombe MP from the train station in 2002. She was due to give a talk on theology at the school. Later that evening, Dad happily agreed to drive the usually loquacious personality all the way back home to the Elephant and Castle. Dad recalls that his passenger fell asleep very quickly on her return journey, so their doubtless cricket-related conversation was, surprisingly, very limited!

Dad was always keen to help out in any way he could, usually helping with the coaching, occasionally umpiring. He recalls umpiring an U14 XI game against Stowe School. Mick Jagger's son was playing for Stowe and was a left-arm medium-pace bowler. They had arrived in his Ferrari, which attracted a lot of attention, unlike Dad's Honda Accord, unsurprisingly! Apparently, one of the Bedford School players hit Jagger's son on to the science block for a huge six, much to the delight of the home team.

During the tea interval, Dad joined some of the parents, including Mick Jagger, and remembers that he enjoyed a few spoons of sugar with his tea: not quite as 'sweet' though, as the strike on to the school building, just before the break!

Bedford School wouldn't insure Dad to drive once he had reached his 70th birthday in 2004, but he still enjoys driving to this very day, when not injured!

Dad went to see his good mate Bob Caple in Johannesburg in 2000. When he returned to England, he bumped into Barry Ebbs in Bedford, who also lived in South Africa, just outside Johannesburg. Barry suggested that Dad to join him in South Africa to watch the World Cup in Cape Town 2003. They had a fantastic time and enjoyed watching the invincible Australian team, never losing a game during the competition and led by the prolific run-scoring Ricky Ponting, which would go on to beat India in the final.

Unfortunately, Barry suffered a stroke in 2004. Dad's caring nature kicked in and he returned to see Barry in 2005 and 2006. They spent six weeks together, talking about their lives, their connections and their passion for the game. Dad remembers Barry pointing out Robin Jackman's house, just around the corner from his own. The Surrey and England cricketer sadly recently passed away at the age of seventy-five, on Christmas Day.

Dad also caught up again with Tony Catt at the Newlands Ground in 2005. They had a couple of beers and reminisced, as they always did. Sadly, Tony passed away in 2018.

Last games
In 2003, Mike Green, who was living in the Moat House, was frequenting the Rowing Club and asked Dad if he could help the Town out by playing against Peterborough. He was concerned that the team would have points deducted for not fielding a full side. Neil Stanley

was skippering and Neil even had to recruit his young son to help with numbers. Dad recalls that Bedford were 'hammered'. Unbelievably Peterborough even had an Aussie 'quickie' playing for them. Dad went into bat as the number 11 and had to face the Aussie. He tells me, with a smile on his face, that he was playing forward when the wicket keeper was throwing the ball back to the bowler!

In 2004, Dad would play another one-off game for Southill Park. Russell Jones had asked Dad to help out at short notice, similar to me 'tapping Dad up' on a Friday evening, back in the late 1990s.

This Southill Park game seemed to bring Dad's cricketing career full circle, as it was at this Bedfordshire ground that Dad has played as a teenager and as one of the Lord's Ground staff.

Unbelievably, when Dad arrived at Southill Park, he realised that, for the first time in his entire cricketing career, he had left his boots at home and thought to himself that perhaps this was the right time to hang them up for good. Russell lent Dad some boots and he went on to take good catch at long off, and a wicket! The wicket he took was the father of an ex-Bedford School boy who was also on the Australian cricket tour in 2004, when Dad had met him previously: small world!

Dad continues to attend the Bedfordshire CCC annual Presidents' Day; last year played at Bedford Modern School. He fondly remembers Arthur Poole. AB Poole was another OBM, who was President in the 1970s. The current President is the charismatic Russell Beard OBM, who has supported the local community in innumerable ways and who had more of a loop with his off-spinners than Dad himself! The well-respected ex-Bedford Town bowler Mike Green was President prior to Russell. Mike, who had succeeded Barry Robinson, played a huge part in the Club's evolution. Prior to Barry, Dad remembers Dudley Wood at the helm.

Russell kindly arranged a mini reunion in the Bedford Club a couple of years ago and Dad had a great catch-up with Rodney Fensome OBM.

During the Presidents' Day games, Dad has enjoyed meeting up with some of the Bedford Town ex-players and recalls catching up with David Pratt, whose son Nick was also a useful keeper/batsman for the club, Chris Whiting, and Peter 'Spike' Findley, among others.

Left the gate open
At my daughter Georgie's ninth birthday in 2008, Dad and Lynn came over to our house in Collingtree Village, near Northampton.

It was a beautiful, sunny afternoon and we had installed the mini cricket set in the garden.

Dad went in to bat, and Georgie bowled. She had a perfect, orthodox slow-arm action and bowled the first ball to Dad on a searching length that Dad would have been proud of. The ball found its way past Dad's blue plastic bat and caught the outside of the off-stump. Georgie punched the air with glee, then apologised and ran to Dad to given him a 'hard luck' hug. Dad simply smiled, and acknowledged that he had been beaten by a wonderfully executed delivery. There was no need for the third umpire and he declared that it wasn't the 'garden gate' that had been left open.

During Dad's playing days, he never once showed any bitterness: he always accepted the umpire's decision and played the game with the integrity it deserved. Perhaps occasionally he would be disappointed, but he was always upbeat and just pleased to be part of the set-up.

Spanish Retreat

In 2006, Dad bought a property in Alcossebre, a beautiful village on the Eastern Mediterranean coast of Spain, not far from Valencia. Lynn's friend Pam has a holiday home in Alcossebre and had mentioned that her neighbour's house had recently been put on the market.

Dad enjoyed the beautiful Spanish retreat, less than a 400-yard walk to the beach, for ten years. He overlooked the welcoming communal swimming pool, accessible to the cluster of properties that were on the Close. He typically travelled over to Spain with Lynn a couple of times a year, in March/April and September/October. During his ownership period a new airport was built, which was ideally situated, being just a twenty-minute car journey away from the village.

Umpires

The legendary John Arlott quote sums up the role of umpires: 'Cricket is a most precarious profession; it is called a team game but, in fact, no one is so lonely as a batsman facing a bowler supported by ten fieldsmen and observed by two umpires to ensure that his error does not go unpunished.'

Dad always enjoyed good, healthy professional relationships with the umpires. On the pitch, their decision prevailed and was respected, even when the 'ball was going under the stumps!'

In the clubhouse, they sat with the players during tea and had a pint or two with them after the game. Occasionally, other players would make their feelings known, perhaps very subtly: 'Pricey what are you drinking . . . a pint of Specsavers?'

From those early Ken McCanlis days, Dad simply upheld the spirit of the game, understood the umpire's role and, over the years, earned mutual respect from the umpiring community. Neutral umpires were latterly introduced to League and Cup games; the impartiality probably helped some players accept the questionable decisions more easily and perhaps avoided lingering resentment in the dressing room for weeks after any particular incident involving a Bedford Town umpire.

Interestingly, Dad would go on to umpire many a game while at Bedford School. The boys were always encouraged to not speak back, nor show any dissent on the pitch, and to respect the decision of the man in the white jacket.

Colin Head was umpire at Bedford Town throughout the decades and would also become the Chairman of the Club's Committee. The Indoor League has a Trophy dedicated to Colin. He had a distinctive south-western accent, being originally from Weymouth in Devon. He was always smartly dressed, was well respected in cricketing circles, and when he spoke you listened. In the field of play, when his index finger was raised, you walked.

Interestingly, Colin's mentor had been the great Ken McCanlis, who had influenced Dad's life massively. Colin had answered an advert in 1960 (*Bedford Town CC looking for an umpire*) and he'd never looked back, developing a superb reputation around the cricketing circuit. Colin would also eventually become club treasurer.

Derek Hammond was a reliable, dedicated umpire and groundsman during the 1960s. Likewise, Don Matthews was a highly thought-of umpire during that period.

Dad recalls Eric Kenworthy, who umpired throughout the 1970s and who drove a distinctive white Saab. One of his hobbies was to park up on the bridge at Junction 13 over the M1 for a bit of car-spotting. Keith Bright also regularly umpired for the Town.

Gordon Dielhemm was another dedicated Bedford Town CC umpire during the 1980s onwards, and his daughter helped out with the scoring.

Ex-Town players who would become more permanent umpires included David Pratt and 'Ernie the Milkman' Dave Price. Both devoted time to the Club beyond their playing days.

Dad fondly remembers the two white jackets, hanging on the dressing room door hooks, with the six various-sized stones in the pocket that had been used for many years. The shape of the stone was irrelevant, what was key was to have six of them.

For the non-league games, most players didn't mind taking turns with the umpiring when they weren't batting. Yes, it provided a position of responsibility and people had to respect your decision. However, it was also an ideal way to gain an insight into what the track was doing and to have a look at what the opposition's bowlers were up to.

Dad remembers when Bedford tried to introduce a bulb in the score box opening, which would be lit by the scorer to acknowledge the umpire's signal. It was probably useful for Morse code purposes, but the equipment was a little unreliable and scorers would simply go back to waving their hands as an acknowledgement.

In 2016, Dad had his 'second' retirement from Bedford School and was awarded a silver tankard and a glass cricket ball mounted on a plinth from the very grateful OBs.

The engraved message from the school reads: '*Peter, many thanks for your hard work and support over the years in the Bedford School Cricket Programme*'.

The engraved message from the OBs states: '*Oakers, thank you from many generations of Bedford School cricketers, for all you have done*'.

I could sense Dad's pride in his tone. Clearly, Bedford School wanted to show their appreciation and affection for Dad's efforts and dedication over the years. He had left his mark, influenced many, was well respected and had established a longstanding reputation for being 'one of their team'; one who tried to make a difference.

This wonderful trademark was a constant throughout Dad's sporting and working life.

Back living in Oakley

Pandemic allowing, Dad likes the occasional pint at the local Oakley Sports Club and makes the short walk most Sunday lunchtimes. He still likes the open air and enjoys taking Millie out for walks, when he and Lynn are entrusted to dog-sit: he just needs to take more care when playing catch with the border collie!

Dad has been living with Lynn for a number of years in Oakley and they are good company for each other. Lynn tells me that Dad makes her laugh, and can also mow the perfect lawn, but that his DIY skills leave a lot to be desired. So, we all agree why he needed to make the most of his vast network of contacts over the years!

The Bedford Arms is also close by, but Dad's light and bitter is cheaper in the Sports Club. Those who know Dad well will recall that getting 'value for money' is important to him. Often, he'll watch the football on their screen and enjoys following Chelsea's exploits with his good friend Martin Smyth. While Dad had been recovering from his garden injury 'in the slips', prior to the second lockdown, Martin had been kindly providing Dad with a lift down to the sports club and even helped to convert the downstairs cupboard into a loo (assisted by local plumber Jamie Worker), as well as doing some work for Alastair, at his Bedfordshire farm. He's another great person who has gone the extra mile to help Dad out at a time of need.

Dad has always enjoyed a feeling of connecting to a larger community: a vast network of social connections outside of the home. He continues to cross paths, hear or read about friends and people that he has touched during his life. A huge swathe of wonderful people has left a positive impact on Dad, similar to finding the sweet spot on your bat and seeing the ball disappear through the covers to the boundary.

Dreams can become reality

Follow your dreams: life will no doubt test your resilience along the way but, as Dad has demonstrated, this will only help to strengthen your character further.

Throughout Dad's lifetime the people around him have influenced his direction of travel. They have engaged him, recommended him, referred him and inspired him to take action. The old proverb 'it's not what you know but who you know' is so true for Dad and was my daughter's apt choice for the title of his book.

Dad retains the ability to tap into a vast, global network of connections, and to create lasting bonds. He manages daily to have a conversation that stimulates him – usually around cricket, perhaps sometimes about football, and sometimes cars. Social contact is the enemy of loneliness.

Even during this current pandemic, there has been little room for social isolation in Dad's world. Indeed, Dad has now had both vaccinations, and upon arrival for his first vaccination in Ampthill Road, Bedford, a lady called Rebecca, who was helping with the co-ordination of patients arriving, recognised Dad through his mask. She was a retired teacher from the Bedford Prep School and relaxed Dad, making him feel comfortable.

As I wrap up this story, Dad has just returned from a 'staycation' to Llandudno, North Wales, with Lynn. They arranged a coach trip and travelled through Colwyn Bay, where Dad played in that three-a-side cricket tournament during 1953, while completing his National Service. They also visited the Marble Church in Bodelwyddan, near Rhyl, to see the graves of the young Canadian soldiers, who sadly lost their lives when rioting for legitimate reasons in the Kinmel Park Army Camp on the 4th and 5th March, 1919. Dad remembers learning about their unfortunate plight when he was based up there during his National Service – despite the Great War having finished, promised ships to take the Canadians home weren't forthcoming and the Camp was ravaged by a deadly virus. The four soldiers who were killed, were only protesting about the situation.

Sadly, a number of Dad's sporting connections are no longer available for selection at the weekend. However, they remain permanently in Dad's heart, allowing him to share cherished memories. They all had an impact on Dad's own journey and like stars on a clear night above the Bury, shine down on him, I'm sure, and watch over him with smiles. There's no doubt that the talented teenagers from the 1950s Lord's Ground staff are forming a beautiful constellation of stars of their own. I would imagine that the Brigadier is in amongst them, with Old Father Time keeping watch, like he always did.

Dad's definitely got loads of overs left in him without question (perhaps not too many quick singles). Now in his 87th year, his social connections have positively left their mark on both his mental wellbeing and physical health, despite the recent diving catch incident!

The number 87 may be considered the 'devil's number:' in Australian cricket (13 short of 100), but Dad thinks positively. In '87 he has treasured memories of the Aussie Chris Linke returning to the UK and linking up with Dad once more, during his enjoyable time with Bedford School. He recalls the two 300-foot chimneys of the Goldington Power Station that could be seen from his beloved Bury and the memorable Queen Alexandra Road property, which were finally demolished and reduced to dust, just like their four huge sister cooling towers the previous year. A huge industrial blot on the local landscape, finally removed in '87. Reasons to be cheerful about the number 87.

For those people who know Dad, worked with him, played cricket with him, I know that you will read this book, reflect, and have smiles on your faces.

So, whether you are a wily off-spinner who thrives on bowling to left-handers 'in the rough', or the possessor of an innate talent, or if you simply have a passion that drives you forward, be sure to make the most of the connections made throughout your lifetime, just like Dad did. They will add so much value to your journey, bring support when needed, guide you when making choices, and inspire you to realise your dreams. Go create your own stories – and good luck.